■ PAPERWORK

PAPERWORK
Contemporary Poems
from the Job

Edited by TOM WAYMAN

HARBOUR PUBLISHING

HARBOUR PUBLISHING CO. LTD.
P.O. Box 219
Madeira Park, BC
Canada V0N 2H0

Cover design by Roger Handling
Typeset in Plantin
Printed and bound in Canada

CANADIAN CATALOGUING IN PUBLICATION DATA

Main entry under title:

Paperwork

ISBN 1-55017-042-2

1. Work – Poetry.   2. Canadian poetry (English) –
20th century.★   3. American poetry – 20th century.
I. Wayman, Tom, 1945–
PS8287.W65P36 1991   C811'.5408'355
PR9195.85.W65P36 1991   C91-091286-6

CONTENTS

■ THE WORK OF LOOKING FOR WORK

■ DEAR FOREMAN

■ CALLING YOU ON MY BREAK

■ WHEN THEY PUSH THE BUTTONS TO RISE

■ ACKNOWLEDGEMENTS

My first and foremost thanks goes to the writers themselves: for their patience, in many cases, with the long gestation of this anthology, and for their help in other significant ways – not the least of which is their willingness to have their poems included in this volume. Gratitude is due, as well, to Art Cuelho of Montana's Seven Buffaloes Press, for his vital work in collecting and publishing North American stories and poems about farm life, and for his assistance with this project. Jim Daniels and Susan Eisenberg both were particularly helpful in referring work writers to send to this anthology. Special thanks, also, to Howard White of Harbour Publishing for his ongoing support of, and participation in, contemporary work writing.

Thanks, too, to Patricia Sloan of Sono Nis Press for permission to reprint poems by Leona Gom and Robert MacLean, and to Caroline Walker of Thistledown Press for permission to reprint "Fire Storm on Mt. Whymper" by Jim Green from *Beyond Here* (Thistledown, 1983), "The Grievance" by Rhona McAdam, from *Creating the Country* (Thistledown, 1989), as well as the poems by Bruce Hunter. "Killbuck: A Poem for Grinders" is reprinted by permission of Louisiana State University Press from *The Glass Hat* by Richard Stransberger. "Public Relations: Delayed Train", "Not a Train", "Graig's Talk" and "In the Brief Intervals" by Erin Mouré, and "Fear of Failure" and "Caught in the News" by Dale Zieroth are reprinted with the permission of Stoddart Publishing Co. Ltd. "Factory Education", "Timers", "Midnight Date" and "Signing" by Jim Daniels are reprinted from *Punching Out*, Wayne State University Press, 1990.

And this book is for: Stephanie Smith.

INTRODUCTION:
Visible Consequences, Invisible Jobs

We live in a society that hides from itself the basis of its existence. North American culture – high and low, popular or elitist – presents almost nowhere the realities of daily work. This collection of poems thus is a light turned on what our society wraps in darkness: the humour, sadness, joy, anger and all the other emotions that accompany our participation in the workforce.

Our jobs form the central and governing core of our lives. Our daily work – be it blue or white collar, paid or unpaid – determines or strongly influences our standard of living, who our friends are, how much time and energy we have left to spend off the job. Our employment determines or strongly influences where we live and what our attitudes are to an enormous range of events, people, objects, environments. No other activity in daily life has more personal consequences for us than the work we do (or are looking for).

Our jobs also re-create each day every aspect of our society. Because we go to work, our fellow citizens are provided with food, shelter and clothing. Through our employment, people are educated and entertained, methods of transportation are organized, children are raised, and much, much more. But an accurate depiction of what occurs in the workforce is overlooked and ignored by virtually every aspect of the surrounding culture. An honest examination of daily work is missing from our movies and television, news media, schools, advertising, fine arts.

Something considered taboo must be happening at the centre of our life – and so at the heart of our society – if our culture is willing to depict endlessly the *consequences* of our jobs, but not to portray the jobs themselves. For example, our literature, in book after book, anthology after anthology, presents a literary portrait of a nation, a society, in which *nobody works*. One possible explanation for this strange fact is that during twelve years of public education, almost no time is devoted to an account of the history and present conditions of employment in North America. What happens to human beings on the job is not considered a topic for major consideration by our school curriculums, even though working is the activity that eventually will occupy most of the waking lives of every student. For example, as Paperwork was in preparation in the fall of 1989, I was sent two new literature textbooks aimed at high schools. Both were organized thematically; one, *Themes on the Journey* (Nelson), identifies what its editor considers the sixteen major themes of "the human journey." These themes include love, death, nature, as well as art, national identity, war. Work is never mentioned. The second collection, *Themes for All Times* (Jesperson Press), identifies seven themes as representing human life "for all times": relationships, faith and belief, conflict, survival, freedom and equality, dealing with today, facing tomorrow. Again, nowhere in this text is daily work worthy of mention, let alone study.

This almost *pathological* avoidance of looking at everyday jobs is just as evident in popular culture. Any trip around the TV dial will reveal a complete absence of anything resembling true depictions of daily employment. Where jobs are shown, such as hospital work or police work, these portrayals are fantasies, romanticizations, trivializations. Police work is not like *Hill Street Blues* or *Miami Vice*, any more than medical employment is like *General Hospital* or *St. Elsewhere*. This can be verified in only a few minutes of conversation with an actual nurse, doctor, lawyer, detective or uniformed officer.

We expect less than honesty from advertising, and we are not disappointed in our expectations when the *source* of advertised products is supposedly presented. My favourite is "The Land of Dairy Queen," the apparent origin of the tasty ice cream snacks. Here images of mounds of chocolate and ice cream obscure entirely the realities of cocoa production in the Third World and minimum wage service jobs here at home. How much more pleasant to imagine a magical origin for the objects sold to us, than to see clearly where things come from.

Avoiding a consciousness of how human beings really spend their lives is not just an interesting sociological or artistic phenomenon. The pervasive taboo against a portrayal of our daily work tangibly *hurts* us.

As a college teacher, I ask my students how many of them, before they selected their course of studies, talked at length to someone doing the job that is the student's career goal. Often half or more of my students have never done this. The taboo against an accurate look at daily work has thus put them in some peril: they are expending considerable time, money, and effort preparing themselves for a job about which they have only the shakiest or most romantic impression. More immediately, our high school students graduate (or they drop out) largely ignorant of what labour laws and regulations protect them in the workforce, and what opportunities and shortcomings are offered by unemployment insurance, workers' compensation, and similar work-related programs. Again, the potential for pain is great. Young people can fall prey to unscrupulous employers by accepting wages, conditions and hours that violate legal standards. Or, where young employees sense that laws are being broken, they are uncertain how to seek redress.

Whether we are young or old, the taboo hurts us by the cultural silence that smothers what happens to us every day on the job. In this eerie quiet, we each feel isolated, uncertain whether we are the only person who responds to our employment as we do. We counter this isolation with "shop talk," gossip about our specific workplace with our immediate peers. But overall, the silence helps keep us from a collective discussion and understanding of the effects our work has on us, and exploring how we might together fundamentally improve our working lives.

As well, the taboo ensures that our culture perceives our contribution to society as insignificant. For the culture of any society establishes a system of values. What is talked about and otherwise portrayed in art, education, entertainment is seen as having value. What a society is silent about is implicitly understood to be without importance or merit. As long as the supermarket tabloids suggest that we worry about the state of Burt and Loni's relationship, rather than consider, say, alternate means of organizing our own daily lives, we are likely to regard ourselves and what happens to us as less important than those figures and events the surrounding culture insists repeatedly are the proper subjects of our attention and concern. For instance, the deaths of seven astronauts are viewed as an international tragedy, and so they are. But why are the deaths of seven miners in a cave-in any less a tragedy? Don't the miners also leave behind spouses, children, unfulfilled hopes and dreams? Why are some individuals so overvalued and the contribution of the majority of us so undervalued?

This situation saps our willingness to act to change our lives for the better. After all, if we're not the important men and women in society, if our contribution to the community is culturally regarded as worthless, why should we speak out or act collectively to improve our lives? And this lack of self-confidence hurts us, because it strikes at the root of democracy. As the social critic Bob Black puts it: "Once you drain the vitality from people at work, they'll likely submit to hierarchy in politics, culture, and everything else."

The poems of this collection, though they were written individually for many different reasons, together break the taboo against a depiction of our real lives and affirm the vital importance of what the majority of us do all day. Using humour, outrage, poignancy and sorrow, the poems celebrate how our work contributes to creating the society in which we all live, and how our jobs shape our individual lives. If film stars, sports idols and politicians were to vanish tomorrow, the world would still be fed, clothed, housed, etc. because of *our* efforts. This is not the message that bombards us daily from TV screens, bill-boards, books, magazines, art exhibits, classrooms. But it is a truth that *Paperwork* proves beyond doubt.

The poems of *Paperwork*, though, are not intended to be an exhaustive or comprehensive look at the new work writing that has begun to appear across North America. Instead, like its predecessor anthology *Going For Coffee* (Harbour Publishing, 1981), *Paperwork* offers a sampling of what I consider the best of the new poetry about jobs and the working life. As with any anthology, then, the selection reflects the strengths and weaknesses of its editor's judgment. My major criterion for including a poem in *Paperwork* – besides literary accomplishment – is that the poem present an *insider*'s view of the work-place. I am convinced that an outsider's vision of a jobsite or other work situation, however sympathetic, lacks the accuracy that the insider brings to the writing. And accuracy is essential to clear thinking – and writing – about daily employment and its human consequences.

Because *Paperwork* shows us jobs with an insider's eye, we find here both extensive use of detail (often detail that only an insider could know) and comedy (since jokes remain a major way the human race gains perspective about its difficulties). A further examination of these and other facets of the emerging work literature can be found in my *Inside Job: Essays on the New Work Writing* (Harbour, 1983).

The poems in *Paperwork* are grouped into eight sections. "Corncobs on the Slag Road" gathers poems concerned with outdoor work; "Something They Claim Can't Be Made" presents poems on women in the paid workforce; "Piece by Piece You Deliver Yourself" offers poems on service work; and the fourth section, "The Work of Looking for Work," deals with unemployment.

"Dear Foreman," the fifth section, is about production work indoors. This is followed by "Calling You on my Break," which contains poems on how jobs affect human relations. The poems of "When They Push the Buttons to Rise" look at work mainly from a managerial perspective, or describe an employee's direct response to that perspective. The final section, "Less Like Ants," focusses on ways we assess and sometimes resist the limitations our work imposes on us. This section, and Paperwork, closes with two poems from the 1983 public sector general strike in B.C. For it is during a general strike, as at no other time, that it becomes absolutely evident that without our work society ceases to function. Not all the words and images of managers or elected officials, nor the fantasies created by advertising or entertainment, can define the world during such an event. Our value and importance are unquestioned.

By their very nature, however, poems resist the set categories I have established here. For example, there are poems about women in paid employment throughout the collection. Assessments of a specific job and/or a working life appear in many sections also. Even my indoor/outdoor distinction is not an exact one: building construction begins outside, for instance, but by the time the last tradespeople are employed, the work is primarily indoors.

So, despite my attempts to slot these poems according to

their major topics, this writing insists that it is multidimensional. Exactly like the human beings who wrote the poems, and the men and women about whom they speak, these poems defy easy generalization and refuse to be narrowly defined. This is part of their power as art and as people. When we look at them, we see as in a mirror our true selves, our real lives. This is not an experience we are used to. We may be exhilarated or depressed, amused or scornful, respectful or enraged at the sight. But until we observe accurately who we are and where we are, we cannot move forward to better our lives. We can shift from one consumer or political fantasy to the next, but that is not the same thing as improving our common existence. It is the gift of these marvellous poems that they show us both our actual present and a door into the future.

TOM WAYMAN
"Appledore"
Winlaw, BC

INVOCATION:
"You Can Keep Your Poetry"

■ **BILL HASTINGS**
  TODD JAILER

Listen to me, college boy, you can
keep your museums and poetry and string quartets
'cause there's nothing more beautiful than
line work. Clamp your jaws together
and listen:
It's a windy night, you're freezing the teeth out
of your zipper in the ten below, working stiff
jointed and dreaming of Acapulco, the truck cab.
Can't keep your footing for the ice, and
even the geese who died to fill your vest
are sorry you answered the call-out tonight.
You drop a connector and curses
take to the air like sparrows who freeze
and fall back dead at your feet.
Finally you slam the SMD fuse home.
Bang! The whole valley lights up below you
where before was unbreathing darkness.
In one of those houses a little girl
stops shivering. Now that's beautiful,
and it's all because of you.

CORNCOBS ON THE SLAG ROAD
Working Outdoors

■ SLAB ON GRADE
CLEM STARCK

At dawn the concrete trucks
are already there: revving their engines,
rumbling and throbbing, one by one
manoeuvring into position.
Enormous insects,
on command
they ooze from their huge revolving abdomens
a thick grey slime.

Insects attending to insects,
the crew fusses over them, nursing wet concrete
into the forms.

Someone to handle the chute,
a couple labourers mucking, one pulling mesh, and two
finishers working the screed rod –
this is called pouring
slab on grade.

What could be flatter or more nondescript
than a concrete slab?
For years people will walk on it,
hardly considering that it was put there
on purpose,
on a Thursday in August
by men on their knees.

■ ME AND MALONEY
CLEM STARCK

Job's nearly over,
me and Maloney all that's left of the crew.
Sunk in the hillside,
hundreds of tons of reinforced concrete
formed in the shape of a drum
ninety-two feet in diameter, eighteen feet deep –
it could be a kiva, or a hat box, or look from the air
like a missile silo.

It could be a storage tank for toxic waste.
It could be a vault to house
the national treasure.

In any case, it's finished,
ready for backfill. Now it's the earth's.

And I'm left with Maloney,
who likes to drink beer after work
and tell stories.
Construction stories. Ex-wife stories. Stories
like how he clubs possums to death with a two-by-four
when he finds them
prowling in back of his warehouse at night.

He laughs, telling the stories.

Maloney quit drinking once.
After a year and nine months he decided he'd rather
die of alcohol
than boredom.

I know what he means. I work
for Maloney Construction.
When it rains we work in the rain. When it snows
we work in the snow.
I am Maloney's right-hand man:
when he laughs I laugh too.

■ DISMANTLING
CLEM STARCK

Call Joel (eves) 623-9765

Smack in the public eye
at Ninth and Van Buren, tearing down
an old house –
"Not demolition, dismantling!" says Joel. Slowly
we make the house disappear.
It takes a few months.
We do this for a living.

'USED LUMBER FOR SALE' –
neat stacks of it on the front lawn
around a dormant forsythia –
shiplap and siding, and over here
we have two-by...
That pile is already sold.

We also have toilets, sinks, remarkable
savings on bent nails,
French doors, free kindling
and more. Lots more.

■

With the roof off
a house looks more like a cathedral,
rafters outlined against the sky.
A pair of ragged priests,
stick by stick we celebrate
nothing. We are making the shape of nothing,
creating
an absence.

And when we have finished,
what will there be at Ninth and Van Buren?
A square of bare earth
where a house was.
Sidewalk. Foundation. Concrete stoop.
Two steps up
and you're there.

■ JOURNEYMAN'S WAGES
CLEM STARCK

To the waters of the Willamette I come
in nearly perfect weather,
Monday morning
traffic backed up at the bridge
a bad sign.
   Be on the job at eight,
boots crunching in gravel;
cinch up the tool belt, string out the cords
to where we left off on Friday –

that stack of old
form lumber, that bucket of rusty bolts
and those two beat-up sawhorses
wait patiently for us.

Gil is still drunk, red-eyed, pretending he's not
and threatening to quit;
Gordon is studying the prints.
Slab floor, tilt-up panels, Glu-lams
and trusses...

Boys, I've got an idea –
instead of a supermarket
why couldn't this be a cathedral?

■ CONCRETE FEVER
KATE BRAID

Seven and one half yards of concrete
and every last pebble in place.
A certain kind of concrete steps
I'd never built before, and
six different patio slopes all having to run
with perfect symmetry
to that one post hole marker
of a drain pipe
and an architect antsy eagle eye for the least mistake
or merely visual flaw.

I worried, I cursed, I adjusted and nailed
and bless my soul
by six o'clock my steps are a grace to behold
and a joy to ascend
and the water from the hoses
of the concrete finisher
rolls sweetly down all those six slopes
and into that bull's-eye drain.
I love water!
I love concrete!
I love the work I did today!

■ RECIPE FOR A SIDEWALK
KATE BRAID

Pouring concrete is just like baking a cake.
The main difference is
that first you build the pans. Call them forms.
Think grand.
Mix the batter with a few simple ingredients:
  one shovel of sand
    one shovel of gravel
      a pinch of cement.

Add water until it looks right.
Depends how you like it.
Can be mixed by hand or with a beater called
a Readi-Mix truck.
Pour into forms and smooth off.
Adjust the heat so it's not too cold,
not too hot. Protect from rain.
Let cook until tomorrow.
Remove the forms and walk on it.

There is one big difference from cakes.
This one will never disappear.
For the rest of your life your kids
will run on the same sidewalk, singing
My mom baked this!

■ ON THE EDGE
BRAD BARBER

At work on a black November morning
nineteen stories high
on the edge.
I'm perched on the rib of a towering concrete skeleton
hammering steel anchor plates to remove the cement scale.

Icy winds blow down from the mountains
prickling me with needles that freeze my fingers.
Clouds swirl off the ocean
burying me in a foggy shroud.

I glance down into the canyon
at the motion far below.
Small rectangles,   cars,
flow through the streets like logs on a river.

On the narrow sidewalk a lone humanoid glides by
round head on box shoulders
arms and legs swinging like pendulums.

I move along the edge
knowing I should wear a safety belt
knowing I can't get the job done fast enough with a belt on
and knowing the boss will get angry if the job takes too long.
Must keep the boss happy
and keep my job.

Alone, I have a chance to think
on every job there are rules,
the number one rule here is   DO NOT SLIP

Then I tell myself, don't hurry too much
you're so close to death.
I'm gambling with my life so I can keep my job.
But the odds are in my favour
as long as I walk with care
and don't forget the danger, don't get tired
or let my mind wander.

I lie down on the cold slab
to keep my centre of gravity low
(Gravity – I think of its force often up here)

After hammering a while
my arms and shoulders get tired.
I look up from my work
office towers all around me.
I look down again to watch a seagull riding the wind.
White head straining forward
grey back and wing stretched taut
bright fan tail that dips slightly sending the animal
into tight arcing turns.

It wheels and soars
on currents of wind that funnel through concrete corridors.

And here am I with a bird's eye view
clinging to the edge.

Sometimes the odds turn
the danger is too great.
So I belt up and tie myself to the building.
I feel safer
with the wide strap of leather around my waist.

But the boss is always watching
and the pressure to produce continues.
Yesterday I was working fast
hanging half over the edge
to reach the end of a post-tensioning cable.
Jerry, the electrician, came up behind me.
"That looks like fun," he said.
"Oh yeah, lots of fun."
"Especially when you're not tied to the building."
I reached behind and felt the limp rope
and carefully slid back onto the solid concrete.

I looked down to the current of movement on the pavement
     far below
I saw myself reach over a little too far   and slip
grasp for a handhold that isn't there
expect a bone-jarring jerk at the end of the safety rope.
And the sickening flight
the fall that lasts into infinity
but ends with a blinding flash of pure pain
followed by freedom from the anxiety of working nineteen
     stories high
on the edge.

■ CONNECTICUT ZEN
DAVID MCKAIN

A carpenter here tells a story
how his Master said,
"Let me see your hammer" –

then sawed two inches off the end,
handing it back, handle first.
"I can see by the way you hold it,
you don't need the part I cut."

At the end of the day,
the same Master Carpenter
gave Gordon a pocketful of nails. "Here,"
he said, "you're new at this trade,
take these home tonight and practise."
Looking back fifty years, Gordon laughs.

We all laugh,
four of us holding hammers, building
a house for my wife and children and me. "Hey,
tonight let's throw a dance to celebrate!"

I look out at where we are,
out in the woods with no walls, no ceilings –
coming from stars and paper lanterns,
the pavilion fills with music.

Gordon saws across his arm, playing fiddle:
heavily comes Rick, heavily comes John –
they stomp their boots on the plywood deck,
they stoop to bow and curtsy in the middle.

Four of us do-si-do,
we whoop and holler,
honouring after lunch.

■ UNLIKE NAPOLEON
JOSEPH MAVIGLIA

Five-foot-two Pasquale has it rough
getting men to follow
simple orders.

He claps his hands, screaming, "*Avanti!*
Asphalt is coming!"

We don't budge, but joke
about his reddening doll-face nose.

"Who is the boss here?
Me or you?" he challenges.

"We are!" we answer
as he throws his clean white hardhat
to the ground.

■ FIRST JOB
JOSEPH MAVIGLIA

Sal never calls it toil or labour.
Each day he swings his pick
hard into earth, moves
heavy chunks with a teasing laugh.

When we break for lunch,
he's the one slapping his thigh,
whistling at girls
and telling the best jokes.

With a long thin nose and yellow teeth, Sal
has little choice in looks,
but as lunch ends
he's first to set his muscles into motion.

"*Ciucciu beddu di stu cori. . .*", his sweet
donkey song,
cuts the air of the job site, swings
his body up and down,
making every move seem simple.

Infected by his casual approach, I try
a song of my own,
and put my back out taking slabs of concrete off a truck.

That night, Sal visits me at home. Smiling,
he shakes his head from side to side, and says,
"You gotta use your muscles right."

11

Back at work two weeks later, Sal stands by.
Making sure I used my legs when lifting,
he moves away and grins, *"Ciucciu beddu."*

> *Ciucciu beddu di stu cori* translates
> from a Calabrian folk song as *Cute*
> *donkey of my heart.*

■ PORTUGUESE JOHN
JOSEPH MAVIGLIA

Portuguese John's blue eyes
haven't seen
Azorian shores in years.

When he talks   the topic's fish
and salted sea.

Other times
he's silent   like at lunchbreak
as he skins
with one long twirl
an apple underneath a shady maple
skins it
with a six-inch blade.

■ WORK SEASON
JOSEPH MAVIGLIA

November   first snowfall
of the season

Eleven men   we worked
through Spring   hot August
and crisp September

patched pot-holed roads
laid new ones
made muscles talk
with pick and rake
shovel and sledge.

                    Thunder cracks.

It might
          it might just be a rainstorm
and the season   will go on.

■ INVERNO (WINTER)
JOSEPH MAVIGLIA

It's hard to sleep in deep cold winter.
Carlo's muscles   bred by labour
stiffen on his bones
as wind spits flurries over barren roads.

To rise today would lead to nothing
more than coffee
and long dreams of summer sun.

Waste eats Carlo's time and only
hope of Spring
gives reason to the icy days.

Carlo shifts his weight   abandons
green dreams   imagined rays
and perks the coffee up
               before his children
               rise busy   in their youth.

■ THE GHOST IN THE GEARS
HOWARD WHITE

Finally starting to get in the swing of this job
after a morning of false starts, near misses and spills
men starting to stand closer to the bucket of my backhoe
trusting me better than I do myself
the machine moves up the slope, slips the load between them,
swoops back in a neat controlled glide, nudges a drum
two guys struggle to move, not knowing they need my help
they smile, one says, "Okay! Now we're cookin!"
The machine moves around me without the intervention of
     thought
my hands flowing over the levers like an expert typist

I reach for the wrong one the machine lurches men leap
for their lives as the one-ton boulder teeters, almost falls
where they were standing, settles safely back.
What the hell? But I know what it was. I reached for swing
and got stabilizer instead, not simply forgetting but
remembering where that lever was on some machine from the
        past.

It happens about once a year, disrupting my unconscious
        motion,
a palpable ghost I strain to identify –
it couldn't be the old rattletrap Case I worked on last
Its broken seat and sharp, neurotic swing motion
that never could be trusted to become instinctive
are too fresh and I'm too conscious of unlearning it.
This was one from earlier, that snuck up on unsuspecting
        instinct
I go over all the backhoes I have been familiar with
like an aging Casanova counting his women –
not so many in fact, I've been more faithful than they
        deserved.

There was the JCB up at Port Hardy, a gutless old girl
with exceptional balance, or Sparrow's John Deere
that had terrific power but kept breaking its extension boom
all of those had pedal swings just like this new 580-D –
couldn't be any of them. Maybe another type of machine
that ¾-yard Koehring dragline up at Mayo had lever swings
big tall ones mounted on the floor that worked so smooth
one way but the other way chattered so bad the whole house
        shook
and rattled its loose plates and the boom wobbled
I still shudder, dreading the spindle will snap and send me
tumbling ass over teakettle down the gorge
praying to finish the season alive – hadn't thought of it since
but all those cable machines had both swings on one lever,
on the right, and the one I just reached for was left
that first old Sherman of Dad's I learned on in the fifties
had lever swings, one on each side with rubber grips
forever in the process of coming off a tiny machine
with a reach that barely exceeded a man's and hoses
sticking out everywhere, you'd be snagging them every move

14

getting showered with boiling oil and once
one rubbed on a battery post till the wire shielding shorted
igniting the spray of hot oil as it showered forth
found myself sitting atop the world's biggest blowtorch
Charlie Hauka was swamping leaning on his muckstick
    beside me
it was Christmas before his eyebrows grew back
you never knew what would happen next
but we built half the town with that machine
coming back to me after thirty years like it was never gone
something kind of nice about that

The men crawl back to their places, standing just as close
as before   grins on their faces
showing

they all believe in ghosts

■ WATCHING WHEELS
JIM McLEAN

gleaming black raincoats
gather in the circle of light
in front of the crane
and back here
in the dark
rain pelts monotonously on my hard hat
sends a river
down the back of my neck
every two minutes

what the hell are they doing?
Jeez, it seems to take forever
to truck a load
when you're stuck in this job
stretched out on the roadbed
watching for a crack of light
between the rail
and the crane's back wheels

not that it isn't important
if the crane tips over

we'll all be down the road
those of us who are still alive

Whatchya doin'?
the voice comes out of the dark
behind me

Christ, it isn't bad enough
lying here on the ground
at two in the morning
soaking wet
I really need this inevitable asshole
rubbernecking in the rain
asking me what I'm doing

Watching wheels I say
not taking my eyes off the rail

after a while
I hear him shrug in the dark
and walk away
his boots crunching on the ballast
toward the friendly light

■ **BY MOONLIGHT**
JIM MCLEAN

the tank cars lie in snow
a school of killer whales
beached on white sands

dressed like eskimos
we've come to land them
with a 200-ton test line

■ **KLIK**
JIM MCLEAN

the apprentice from Winnipeg
couldn't stand klik

whenever he found
the marbled pink meat sandwiches
in his lunch kit
he would throw them in the garbage
work the rest of the day
on fruit
tormented by the memory
of lunches mother used to make
peanut butter   bacon & tomato
egg salad

the apprentice from Winnipeg
hated klik

too shy to tell the woman
who packed his lunch each day
he made the mistake
of telling us
and every evening after work
carried home in his lunch pail
a note to his landlady
in bold enthusiastic letters

more klik!
love that klik!

■ I DON'T WRITE POEMS FOR RAILROADERS
JIM McLEAN

"I've seen these bitter verses, over
and over again, scrawled on the sides
of box cars."

I don't write poems
for railroaders
they'd use them
to line their overshoes
roll them in balls
to plug their ears   against
those lonely crossing whistles
that make folk singers rich

up hill slow
down hill fast
tonnage first
safety last

they have learned
about the unions
the lies of government
and how the company
will spend five hundred dollars
to avoid paying
a dollar-forty meal ticket

drive those spikes
and don't complain
you don't get hired
for your brain

they spend
lives
along the snow fence
or in the shops
linked
shift to shift
year to year
father to son
they become the rails
lie down beneath the wheels

broken strikes
and broken tools
dirt and death
and books of rules

the smell of creosote
the gleaming yards at sunrise
the trembling power
of the diesels
are the poems
railroaders hold inside

they talk
of the day when they can leave
and stay
unable to go
unable to embrace
the thing
they love

■ THROWING A SHOE
Todd Jailer

Heat rises from the asphalt
in waves given substance by sweat
pouring off my body. Ice
in the water keg long since
melted, four hours on the jackhammer
opens four foot of rock hole.

This is the payback for questions
at yesterday's safety meeting.

Charlie shouts through the ringing
in my ears, I can't make out
a word, I nod in agreement.
Wedged in a stubborn crevice of quartz,
a little too much pressure,
a facile shoulder twist, and
Crack – the last digging bar breaks.
Charlie smacks the 2-way radio,
a crescent wrench between the eyes,
all mumbling ceases. We try
to raise the foreman: sullen
silence. Lying in the grass,
redeemed within the jaws
of heat, we bless Joy Manufacturing,
maker of faulty jackhammers.

■ MOTTO OF THE LINE CREWS
Todd Jailer

Ours is not to fret or worry
But to stay here 'til 4:30.

■ I'M DRIVING
TODD JAILER

I'm driving the bucket
truck to the job when
the new helper asks,
"How come the birds
on the wires don't get
electrocuted?" I down-
shift into second and
yell over the engine
"Rubber feet." He nods
in understanding as
I watch from the corner
of my eye, measure
his developing suspicion
against the memory
of my own.

■ IN LOCO CITATO
TIMOTHY RUSSELL

Deer still on the island venture
onto the slag perimeter road
to feed on corn thrown down
by the payloader operator.
The deer are not cunning.
This is simply the way it is
between them. I understand
this is not an experiment.

The spotlight of a tug
shoving barges upstream
sweeps the river
catches for an instant
a few deer on the island feeding
one or two of them looking up.
The light veers from bank to bank
but always returns to the herd
as if whoever is at the light
doubts the deer exist.
The boat moves one way.

The river flows the other.
The deer continue feeding.
This is simply the way it is.

The operator knows deer
linger on the island.
He drops corn for them
or apples or whatever he has.
He sees the yellow deck-lights
of tugs on the river. At night
he loads conveyors with coke.
Although he works alone
building the huge coke piles
he is not lonely. He sees
the beam sweeping back and forth
across the river. He sees it stop.

Deer still on the island venture
onto the slag perimeter road
to feed on ears of corn. Sometimes
truck drivers from the mainland plant
cross the bridge to the island
hoping to see a few deer.

A truck crosses the bridge
moves along the idle battery
past the quencher that never really worked
past the empty and quiet payloader
past the inclined conveyors.
The truck stops long enough
for a passenger to get out.
I have to bleed the propane
from a defective cylinder.
I walk over to the river.
A tire floats downstream.
The river is high and muddy.
I wonder how fresh the deer tracks are
have barely enough time to look up
and see five or six deer stumbling
through the brush. Later
with propane still leaking
I find corncobs on the slag road.

■ WALHALLA, NORTH DAKOTA
WILLIAM BORDEN

On the prairie,
in March,
patches of moisture
speckle the fields
as if the earth
were working up a sweat,
getting ready.

■ RIPPIN' WITH THE "8"
FRANK CROSS

Just started, idling,
The engine was rumbling,
Its six big pistons pumping,
Floating on oil.
He shoved ahead
The long clutch lever,
Held it forward
To brake the gears.
His right hand
Grabbed the heavy
Gearshift lever and
Bounced it off
The teeth of second gear.
Finally the lever dropped in
And he shoved the throttle
All the way open.
Black smoke boiled out the stack.
The turbo caught hold
And the stack cleared
As he eased the
Clutch lever back.
Tension building,
Discs began to turn,
Gears passed the power back
Tooth to tooth.
The sprockets bit track chain,
And he snapped the clutch over centre.
The big tractor began laying track.

He yanked the hydraulic lever
Full open and the ripper teeth
Sank slowly below the surface.
Deeper and deeper they sank,
Down to the beam.
The hard soil rose up,
Shattered behind and
The machine clanked mindlessly on.

ON HEARING THAT EZRA BECKER WAS KILLED WHILE PLOWING

CRAIG CHALLENDER

He must have fallen asleep.
Day warm as blood,
windless trees, tractor
thrum, throb, hum
of summer: beyond hedgerow
hay-scent, blooming butterflies.

And so much land to work.
You know how it goes —
those twelve-hour days, your hands smudged
black; the time comes when iced
coffee won't work, when gull-flights
circle through your eyes, pulling
them downward. The headland's
a soft smudge in the diesel fumes.
The land furrows your brows, snakes out black
behind you, and underneath you can feel it
pulse, feel it pull, sending
shudders through your front wheels.
Then's when you breathe it out,
like a breeze rippling green wheat:
"It's mine, and ain't it pretty."
And behind you you can hear the shares whisper.

So he fell, asleep. His last
startled view of things
was not the dust-coloured
stubble, the hedge's burned
green, or even the blue

blankness of the sky: for him
instead the seat's sieve
holes, power take-off
slowly circling...tool
box...manure-flecked
fenders...and finally, overhead
the cranks and ropes. Blood
starts, shoots: the field
folds in Ezra Becker
like a hidden dream.

So he must have gone –
a clenched seed, recalling
the hard red of the buckberry.
The fist flowers fingers.

■ NIGHT HARVESTING
RICHARD HOLINGER

To go night harvesting, son,
you have to know your field's
rows, bends, rises, limits,
because when the dark approaches
you're more easily taken away
than when running in the light,
more easily lost to the music,
or to the squeals of animals
snapped in with the corn.

You feel the field.
Follow your stalks, the rods
brown as light as tobacco leaves,
like a sniffing dog with steel fangs.
You'll feel a quiver
when the crisp-kerneled cobs crack.

You can't reap it fast enough –
that's why you're out here now,
because nights thicken with cold
and narrow days to strings too short
to tie in crops when their time

comes; even though time changes,
you can't avoid the dark.

Here are your lights. Use them
with dusk (don't wait for stars),
when houses behind your last field
all look grey as the smoke
their leaves have burned,
when the fires look like warning flares
left in front of empty homes.
To people inside, you will be
a wide-eyed beast devouring life
which to them looks gone,
a monster to frighten children's
dreams on Halloween:

you have been let loose
to cut through what you can.

■ HARVEST AT NIGHT
JANET KAUFFMAN

If the dead were to rise up in blasts
of dust and engine noise, unchoired,
we would shout this same way, unsure
our words could travel through air.
In the cornfield, stalks catastrophically
ghost to silver, flowering headdresses, flags.
Each stalk – an ancient, pale man; a husk –
becomes ceremonial scrap, and the multitudes
enter the harvester's light; row after row
they rattle to each side, and breaking, fall.
The work of machinery shows nothing new.
Deer, too, in this field, see in the dark
the world, with phantasmal arms, part.

■ HANDS
LINDA HASSELSTROM

The words won't come right from my hands
or brain in spring. The fields are full
of baby calves, tufts of hay, bawling cows.

My brain is full – but words won't come.
Sometimes when I'm in the truck,
leading heifers to spring grass, I find a stub
of pencil, tear a piece from a cake sack,
and make notes, listening to the curlews'
wolf whistle. A barb tore that knuckle,
shutting a gate without my gloves. The blood
blister came when someone slammed a gate
on the branding table; I tore the fingernail
fixing a flat. The poems are in the scars,
and in what I will recall of all this, when
my hands are too broken to do it anymore.
Instead of a pencil my hands,
knotted like old wood, grip a pitchfork,
pitching hay to cows; blister
on the handles of a tiller. Slick
with milk and slobber, they hold a calf,
push the cow's teat into his mouth,
feel his sharp teeth cut my fingers –
another scar. From my hands pours cake
for the yearlings, seed for garden
that will feed my family.

My hands become my husband's, weathering
into this job he chose by choosing me; my father's
broken and weathered, still strong as when
he held me on my first horse.
At night, while my body sleeps, my hands
keep weaving some pattern I do not recognize:
waving to blackbirds and meadowlarks,
skinning a dead calf, picking hay seeds from my hair
and underwear, building fires. Deftly, they butcher
a chicken with skill my brain does not recall.

Maybe they are no longer mine but grandmother's,
back from the grave with knowledge in their bones
and sinews, hands scarred as the earth they came from
and to which they have returned.

When my grandmother was dying, when
the body and brain were nearly still
for the first time in eighty years, she snatched

the tubes from her arms. At the end,
her hands wove the air, setting the table,
feeding farmhands, sewing patches. Her hands kept
weaving the air,
weaving the strands
she took with her
into the dark.

■ SALVAGE GRAIN
David Lee

1
On the way to the feedstore
John sez we oughta be able to get the grain
for two dollars and so when the man bid
two and a quarter I sez that's that
and John moves behind Jan and whispers
bid two thirty and I sez what?
and he winks and I bid and the man bid
two and a half and John calls him a sonofabitch
to Jan and the other man looks at me
to see if I'll bid and I shake my head no
and John he punches me and sez three
and I sez what? and he sez three
and I sez three and the man calls me
a sonofabitch to his wife and the other man sez
what's your name and John sez tell him Homer
and I sez what? and John winks again and I sez
Homer Melvin because that's all I can think
and he tells the secretary to put down Homer
for ten tons and we go home.

2
A month later the man calls John
and sez where's Homer Melvin? and John sez
oh him? he died and the man sez but
he bought all this grain and what am I going to do
and John sez damn he's sorry he don't know
but he'd take it off his hands for two dollars
a hundred and the man sez no and hangs up
but calls John back in an hour and sez
come get it and John calls me

27

and I get Jan to write a check for two hundred
for our half and we go to meet John to go
to the feedstore and the man looks at me funny
and sez what's your name and I say Dave
and he sez isatso? and John sez you damn right
he's Dave what'd you think I made him
my partner for? and we load our two dollar
grain in John's and my truck and go home.

■ RACEHOGS
David Lee

John calls and sez Dave
when I say hello and I say hello John
and he sez come down Dave
you gotta see what I got
I say fine I'll be right there and he sez
bring Jan I'll show her too
and I said I will
so Jan and I got in the car to see
what John bought.

John bought four hogs
starved half to death, bones out
everywhere, snouts sharp enough
to root pine trees and the longest damn legs
I've seen. What do you think? he sez
and I don't say anything so he sez
I sez what do you think? and I say
them's pretty good-looking racehogs John
and he sez what? and I tell him
I heard about a place in Japan or California
(because he's never been there) where they
have a track and race hogs
on Tuesday nights and he sez do they
pay much? and I say yes or so I heard
maybe a hundred to win and he sez
goddam and I say those hogs
ought to be good with them long legs
and skinny bodies and he sez goddam.

Jan's walked off so I go find her
but she's mad and says I ought not to do that
and I say oh I was just bullshitting
but when we come back John's standing
by the fence throwing little pieces of feed
all around the pen making the hogs
hurry from one place to the next
and when I get up close he's smiling
and I can hear him whisper
while he throws the feed
run you skinny fuckers, run.

A DAY OF MOURNING,
24 NOVEMBER 75
DAVID LEE

I had to sell my black sow Blackula today.
She has become fallow, rejects the boar,
has no pigs and eats too much to keep.
Alas, goddammit, I loved that pig.

THE HAY SWATHER
DAVID LEE

Dave John sez Dave is that you?
I sed hello John
John sez it's that damn swoker I bought
I sed did something go wrong arredy?
John sez yas so I sed but you just got it
it shouldn't break down that quick
was it bad? Goddam John sez
it busted all to hell
the manifold bushings mebbe a flywheel bearing
it could of been the drive shaft or cam I dunno
I tried to fix it and climbed underneath and beat it
with the hammer so when I went to start it up
the clutch jerked a knot in hisself
and felt across the ground
I had a hundred more acres of hay I told him
I'd knock down before weekend
and I didn't even have a dog with me

to kick his ast
it wasn't nothing I could do but stand and watch

I sed John I don't know anything
about machinery John sez whar?
I sed nowhere
John sez oh well that don't matter now
so I sed that's good
John sez if I could of found him I'd of
loosen up his hide right now
I sed whose? John sez
the one that solt me the swoker who you talking about?
I sed oh him
John sez yas but it was too late
sos I went home and made up these words
I practised what to say in the night
next morning I got my truck and drove
to the crossroads before I got there I stopped
and put some of the words on my hand
sos I wouldn't be lost when I got mad
and if I hit him I'd have them all right there
he'd know how come
cause he was gone say well John I be damn
I'm sorry but it was a used one and all
there ain't nothing he can do

I pulled up and he's standing right there
eating a sandwich for breakfast
and sez hello John I sez I gotta talk to you

right now he sez you want a sandwich
he hadn't had his breakfast yet
I sez no I ain't got no time to eat a sandwich
I'd eat a cupcake and a can of viennies
on the way so he sez come in
we went in his office and set down
I lain my hand out on the table sos I could
see the words I sez listen here
that swoker you solt me done busted all to hell
and it ain't been that long
and you ought to do something about it
it ain't right that way

I didn't say or I'll whup your ast
but I had it wrote down
if I needed it for later

he didn't say nothing
he picked up the phone I thot he's calling
the law mebbe but he sez Roy
tell Bubba unload that big truck to somebody
and he sez yeah now
I'll need it this morning sos he hangs up
the phone he sez John well
it's only one thing I can do
we'll go load up my swoker and take it out
to your place sos you won't lose no time
and load yours up and I'll bring it back
and fix her up cause I guarantee it
all I sell for ninety days
if it busted reckon it's my fault not yours
so what else can I do for you this morning?

I sed John what'd you say?
John sez I looked at my hand
and I ain't wrote nothing for that
so I sez that sandwich sounds fine
it's all I could think of
and I wasn't even hungry
I couldn't shake his hand
cause he might see them words I put on it
I never thought he'd go and say
something like that
and I couldn't just set there
so he torn his in half and we both
eat a piece waiting

■ **THE FARM**
  DAVID LEE

We sold it. To a man
who would be a patriarch.
I told John we were closed in,
subdivisions and trailers all around,
complaints of the smell (though

there was none), Ira came out
and told me to keep them fenced
(though none broke out), the neighbours
frightened because someone's cousin's
friend heard of a hog
that ate a child who fell in the pen (though
their children rode my sows
at feeding time), because I was tired,
because Jan carried our child and could
no longer help, because she wanted a home.

And the patriarch lost his first crop
to weeds, threw a rod in the tractor,
dug a basement and moved the trailer on
for extra bedrooms, cut the water lines
for a ditch, subdivided the farm
and sold the pigs for sausage. I told John
they were his, they were no longer mine,
I couldn't be responsible.

The wire connecting our voices was silent
for a moment. "You stupid sonofabitch," was all
he finally said. "You poor stupid bastard."

■ SOME THINGS WORK
STEPHEN LEWANDOWSKI

We use the horse to haul out wood.
He farts before he pulls.
You won't find a tractor'll do that.
The season's too wet for tractors –
they just dig themselves a hole.
All the farmers bitch about their crops,
lost or delayed, puddles in the corn
rows & beans turning black with mould.
But the horse pulls real nice & a load
of sound deadfall elm & lively hickory
slides up the ½-mile hill to the house.
We buzz up the logs, split the biggest
with ax and maul, stove-size.
Some people might get a kick
out of our stone-boat:

dark blue volkswagen hood & chain,
but it holds what a horse can pull
& slips right over the grass
in the low, wet spots.
It works & we work & later
we sit before the fire.

▎ I'M SO LONESOME IN THE SADDLE SINCE MY HORSE DIED
SID MARTY

for D.L.

"Well, he rode the bush rodeos.
He was sure enough a cowboy,
he was a hand.

God he was rank, though!
Always ridin' his horse through some bar,
such a tired old trick.

He done that in Cochrane.
Comes chargin' thru the pickups out front
and right through the front door.
And if he wasn't doin' it,
he was holdin' the door
for some other rangy-tang.

One time he rode in with his lariat –
roped guys right outta their chairs
skidded them into the parking lot like calves...

Boy they was hungry for him that day!
All them drugstore cowboys from Calgary,
chased him with trucks all over town
That horse jumpin' fences and
him duckin' clotheslines
with bedsheets and pantyhose
strung around his neck.
That was a pretty tame mount he had
that time, I tell yuh.

They call 'em 'urban cowboys' now,
yuh know. Shee-it!
Buncha drunken half-ton jockeys
all duded up in their Rexall regalia,
they couldn't cut 'im off,
just smashed each other up instead,
at every corner.
He made it to the river
and hid out in the trees.

Ain't it strange
how well some men can ride
yet never make good horsemen.

He treated horses like he hated 'em.

I disremember when it was
he bought this mighty gelding, Boots.
That pony really threw the honkytonk
on Jim, he could not stay aboard.

So he tripped old Boots
with a Scotch hobble.
Yuh know he kept that pony down
until its hooves came near
t' fallin' off.

I always suspicioned him to be
'bout two bricks short of a load
but that was a bit too western for me.

Old Boots was about ruined.
'Fox the sonmuhbitch then,'
says Jim.
'He'll make some dog sick.'
(He didn't like dogs, either)

His wife, though, she was a wonderful woman,
a big skookum girl from Spillamacheen
but a beauty.

Never asked for much, 'cept once.
She wanted a TV. Well, he bought her one
in town, threw it in the truck
and proceeds home, drunk
which was his rule
over Texas gates
at amazin' speeds...

Natchrally the set
got bucked into the tulies...
But he gathered up the remains
and when he got home
dumped this junk on the floor, says
'There's yer TV, hon.
It's a colour one, too.'

And he laughed, that fool.
Figured it was a helluva joke.

She never left him, though.
What a woman sees in a man like that,
I'll never know.

Guess he met his Waterloo
in the Caroline Hotel
– some big roughneck dismounted him real hard.
A month of hospital rations kinda tamed him down...

Next I heard, they'd moved to Utah.
Guess he was a bit ashamed of it all.
He was born too late, yuh see,
for the time he was livin'.

Like when we was ropin' cows,
he'd never wear gloves...
He says 'They never wore gloves, the old guys.'
Well jeez you know they couldn't afford 'em, probably!
His hands was like hamburger, but he'd say,
'The only thing yuh can do well with gloves on
is shit yer pants.'

He wouldn't even wrap the horn with rubber
to take the dallies. The old timers never
used that, either. 'Well you dipstick,'
I told him, 'they didn't have it to use, is why.'
All they had was that shaganappi, rawhide.

Then he'd tag some old bitch of a Hereford,
and he'd burn them hands, Lordy!
Make yuh cringe to see it . . .

Just a big stubborn kid all his days
Livin' in the past
he never knew,
gettin' it wrong all the time.

Maybe that's what it was
with her. Some women love a loser . . .

Anyway, he was sure enough
aw-thentic cowboy.

He was a hand."

■ DANGEROUS WORK
PETER CHRISTENSEN

I turn to dangerous work
as a soldier turns to war
his body a divine target
testing luck over skill.

Hanging my life from ropes,
hoping the wild card
of friendship will surface
I think back to love
back to the pornography of
the body politic
the exhibition of our desires
the graphic conclusion of animals
these if any, will be
my last thoughts.

Above me a massive snowslab
hangs
suspended in the tension of particles.
The world surrounds me
but fear bursts the veil.
In stones, stress and
the humpback knowledge of machines
working the pit below
my nerve unfolds trust
is
until forever   dangerous.

STOPPING BY THE WOODS ON A SNOWY EVENING
PETER CHRISTENSEN

My rifle in hand
I listen for an animal
Am tall among the young pines.

On the dark side
Of a ravine I wait
In a cold white shadow,
Watch the barren hillside.

I the impatient hunter.
I wait for an animal.
I write poetry.

As the light fades
I find the path to home,
Unload the rifle.
Cartridges lie in my pocket
Like patient slaves.

SWAMP KING
SID MARTY

for Perry

We thought he was a rogue black bear
A savage runt, the mauler of four:

37

one man blinded, one clawed up
one died later in the doctor's care

That was the worst,
and then the fourth man
shortcut the warning signs
that closed the swamp

In the dark willow bush
he met the bear head on
and crawled out, half scalped
over beaver dams to the road
With the blackrobed
Justice of the Peace
growling at his heels

"He was black, pure black!"

The Indians at Morley said he was a spirit bear
I think they prayed for him
They asked us for his body, for their rites.

Some thought he was senile
Some that he had a tapeworm
"Or maybe he's got a dead pilgrim in there
waiting for him to ripen"

And the summer help sat in the pubs
talking knowingly about imported bears
brought in to draw the tourists
A chamber of commerce plot

But the bear stayed in his swamp
and said nothing
It was his court
and the moves were all his

In the swamp the birds sang
oblivious to tragedy
The tracks of black bears
covered everything
There was a bear for every tree

Around the swamp, we stood with rifles
while snares were set, baited with beaver meat

The swamp went crazy, fighting for our offerings
And in the dark, the black bears came out, running,
like rabbits leaving a fire
First the little ones, then the large

Brief shadows between the headlights
No way to shoot, and a good thing, too.

For in the dark heart of willows
there was a cry
of unbearable sadness and fury

Next morning, in the snare
we found him
He was black, all right
A coal black grizzly
over 700 pounds
caught in the half-inch cable
by the right front foot

He'd carved a crater in the mud
with his free paw
Bit down trees eight inches through
waiting for us to come to him

Afterwards, measuring our pygmy hands
against his armoured foot
we said he was a gentle bear
because he pulled his punches
defending a hunting ground

Though when he came
for his executioners
beckoning them closer
with his five-inch-long claws

He hit his tether so hard
that the trees trembled in pain
and leaves fluttered to earth

He rolled with the bullet
in his skull
But stood up on his hind feet
up
and up
shaking his head
at the insult of that lead bee

Came down like a bomb
exploding in the flying dirt
toward the sound of shotguns

Holding his five front talons
out like supplicating, ivory fingers

Falling and getting up
Falling and getting up.

Science took the body
slung from a helicopter
swaying slowly in the breeze

One of the shooters clipped
his daggers for a necklace

The noise of the traffic
never stops, along that road
But after a while
the birds began to sing again

■ FIRE STORM ON MOUNT WHYMPER
JIM GREEN

1
"Marble Canyon's going up;
if we don't get rain we're done for,
she'll rampage down the valley
clear to the Province."

Now that sounded serious
but hard to believe.
It meant the Bow Valley

would blaze up in smoke,
Banff, Canmore, and Exshaw
wither and succumb
and Calgary
burn down before the Stampede.

The sun burned
red through the smoke haze
above Banff Avenue.
Smoke crept around Rundle
to blanket Canmore.

It was west of Storm Mountain
where lightning struck an old snag,
small flames fermented and blossomed.
Fire ravaged the east side of Whymper,
was about to swallow Marble Canyon.
Cats were trucked fast to the fire line;
spotter planes, bombers, and choppers
were already backing the ground crews.

The cops knew how to get fire fighters.
Pulling up in front of the bar,
they waited for a while in the car;
then taking their time
and the volunteer roll,
they'd stroll right in
looking for customers.
Those that were left had excuses,
obligations, complications, and reasons,
or they would be only too happy, sir,
to stomp right out and do their duty.
The routine was not all in vain.
At the rear door was a touring bus
backed up tight to the wall
where two husky horsemen

were double arming the anxious
to a seat and a trip up the mountain.

In the morning,
waking up hung over and sickly,

rolling from grey blankets,
cursing the cold and their luck.
Red-eyed, stiff-backed, and big-headed,
squinting through the hot smoke,
blinking at the mountains of hose,
the stacks of axes and the shovels.

2

Hose over one shoulder
clenched tight in both fists
I'm dragging it uphill   upmountain
breath coming in hot rasps
sweat dripping into both eyes
my hard hat keeps slamming
whack   down onto my nose.

A mile and a half of canvas we need
to push water up from the river
one heavy duty pump   two relays
to reach the line.   Check grease
twist on the coupling   prime pump
yank starter rope   yank it again
again   it fires.   Water swells canvas
balloons the hose writhing upmountain
to the crew anxious in smoke.

Air choked with flying black needles
burnt crisp and feather light
flooding into mouth
filling nose and throat
or landing red hot
burning small crescents
on clothes.   Lungs
simmer till they hurt,
hot ground burns feet
eyes water
back is sore
legs are tired –
the pumps are all hammering
hoses swollen hard
there's water up there now

and   about bloody time
the truck with the chow.

3

We've strung hose along a new slash
half a mile   above the river
the fire's roaring in on two of us
standing there   waiting for water
holding the hoses limp
bug-eyed   scared as hell
ready to run from the flames.

A spotter plane darts in low
for once things work as they should:
a bomber dips in on target.
Water bomb slams towering fire wall
and we are lost
in a swirl of hot fog.
Then   in bops a chopper
and fearing the sticky pink mud
we are ready again to run
but smile to welcome the water
splashing heads and hot shoulders.

The hose twitches   goes stiff
water rushes the T-joint
gushes out my nozzle and his.
We turn the jets on each other
shower spray on upturned faces
soaking wet and screaming
laughing off the fear

4

The wind switched   blew back on the fire
it rained lightly that night
and steadily the next morning.
The line was held   pushed back
only a few spot fires left.

We'd manned that line the long night
flares winking red all around.
Dawn found us drained and hungry

so we quit for coffee and breakfast
some sleep in the morning light.

Sharpened sticks shoved in soft soil
draped with wet socks   shirts
steaming upside-down boots
a strange cluster of totems
around a smouldering cook fire
in the burn above Tokumn Creek.
We were sprawled on our bellies
and backs near the fire
waiting for the coffee to boil
dozing on the warm ground.

Camped by the loud creek
under black brush and spruce trunks
we didn't see it   or hear it
till too late
or too tired to care.
But it was far too late
when we scrambled wildly
dived for heavier cover
as the shadow bore down on us
jettisoned its load.

The chopper pilot was an ace
scored a dead centre hit
blasted ashes into black faces
busted coffee pot and pack boards
scattered laundry and footgear
wiped out that camp fire for good.

WE COME TO ASK FOR YOUR BONES
Cutting the Great Fragrant Western Red Cedar
MIKE O'CONNOR

for Steve Conca

The first thing we do:
clear the brush and wiry limbs
back from the flaring butt
and look up.

I tap the trunk with my axehandle
and the top answers
200 feet in the blue;
then hugging it, reckon the lean.

I stand back and ask you who to cut;
you grin and say, so I reach around
and make the lower portion of the undercut
straight in till I think I might hit rot;
then the upper portion at 45 degrees and
kick the wedge-shaped block out;
stand back, look up,
kill saw and figure the backcut.

Now this is a big tree for the Rainshadow,
and a 36-inch bar is nice to have,
and a powerhead that blows your ears off
(use a little wax or cotton).
That distant top is barbed like devils club
and non-regulation caps are crazy
(forgot my hardhat, thought we were going fishing).
Tap the tree, make sure it's still one piece.

You got the wedges – what am I doing here? –
put the saw across the swell and go
through the blue exhaust that floats among the maples,
through jets of sawdust warm as blood.
Jam the plastic wedge in deep;
I'm where the rot must start.
She tips a little;
click off saw and find a place to run.

She's talkin', she's crackin'
in the check but will not fall.

We freeze, like game in someone's sights.
Back under her again, you tap the wedge
and give it one firm bust
and then another:

slower than a rising star
the butt begins to turn across the stump,

and then she's free!

Chainsaw and sacklunch and find a place to fly,
we've cut the ridgepole that supports the sky.

And the brittle Goddess – after standing dead
and silver fifty years – like a wave
begins to break upon the rocks.

Barbtop whipping like a fly pole
splinters into stars; the accelerating stem explodes
the crown of a maple; pauses momently
in the whirl of greenery, slams a big Doug fir,
blazes down its side, pounds into the earth,
recoils, lurches sideways and falls still.

A clap of thunder echoes through the hills.
A conky chokecherry floats out from the shade
and bursts beside us.

Limbs, sprays...
then only thousands of needles
raining in our hair, on the fern
and honeysuckle earth, on the silent cedar hulk.

We get to our feet. The sun streams through
the thinned canopy. Steve is making
one of his wide-eyed, Holy Jesus-what-was-
that-all-about faces,
then says, "Holy Jesus, what..."

laughs and hands me the Copenhagen.
"Except for the maple, Doug fir,
woodpeckers, squirrels, etc., I think
you dropped her just about right."

We clamber up the high and hollow stump to look:

lots of taper wood and nothing serious in fractures.
Then a short leap, and we are walking,

       walking the length of her lovely bones.

■ THE FINISHING
PETER TROWER

Last day   last hour   last log
big grizzled fir butt
lead-heavy with pitch   seesawing
on the lip of a hundred-foot hole
There's two or three more good pieces
down in that spooky pit –
they can damn well stay there –
only a chopper could harvest those bastards.

Last day   last hour   last log
I take my time with it   easing
ragged cable around rough bark
in the too-familiar ritual
I punch the whistle   the choker snaps taut
the fir butt shakes alive
shudders up from its death bed
crunches toward the spar tree.

Last day   last hour   last log
a sense of relief   a sense of sadness
now I will run in the lines and blocks –
we have had our way with this mountain
Another woodwar won
another forest felled and stolen
another notch on some timber king's desk
another virgin hill ahead of us.

■ COLLISION COURSE
PETER TROWER

It is a tree of average girth
neither the tallest nor the smallest
it has rolled with the punches
of a hundred mountain storms
and weathered every one.

He is the sort of fastidious faller
who mixes his gas with a measuring-cup
his boots are carefully greased

they crunch through the remnant snow
he carries the powersaw casually like a suitcase.

The tree shudders
as the chain rips through its growth-rings
the man guides his tool impassively
thinking about his wife and kids
chips spray like shrapnel
the engine growls like a wounded cougar
fibres part before blurring teeth
the tree quakes   begins to inch
unwillingly from the vertical

The man withdraws the saw   snaps it silent
leans against a stump   gropes for a smoke
on a tearing hinge of wood
the tree tips   hisses down
but the faller's aim has been faulty
the hemlock strikes a standing cedar
the butt breaks free   kicks back
like a triggered piston.

There is no time to run
the butt connects like a wooden hoof
pins the man to the stump
his ribs snap like sticks
fastidious to the end
he pulls free his wallet
places it safely above the blood
on the tree that has felled him.

■ GOOSEQUILL SNAGS
PETER TROWER

Barney Cotter
bought it up in Ramsay Arm
Read it in the papers
twelve years back
Wild log rolling-pinned on him
crushed him against a rock.

Barney and I worked together
in Halsam's camp on Goatfoot Mountain
with his chattering chuckle
that broke to a graveyard cough
hurting his way ahead of me up the slopes
burned out from booze and board feet at forty-five

Barney was philosophical
"That's the name of the game" he'd say
squinting out from under his hard hat
firing another cigarette
"Always wanted to run a store or somethin'.
But I ended up a goddam logger!"

There were a lot of dead trees on that claim
hollow fire-gutted cedar shells
spiking up among the felled timber
"Goosequill snags" Barney called them
I never forgot the term
It was his only poetry.

Barney is long buried
but his goosequill snags still stand
on the mending slopes of Goatfoot Mountain
monuments
to another man the hills took
writing his rough legend on the sky.

■ **TRIMMING THE TREE**
DAVID MCKAIN

Machete-whacking in November,
I cull out the deadwood,
releasing cedars: in January
I order blue spruce and fir
in bundles of two-fifty,
each seedling big as a sprig.

I plant them in April,
four feet apart in a clearing –
it takes eight years of sun and rain
to grow a Christmas tree,

average soil, an occasional pruning,
a slow scythe between each row.

A foot a year sounds simple,
though the state's advice is, buy
herbicides, insecticides
and poison bait to kill the mice:
kill the crabgrass,
the pigweed and the shepherd's-purse,
and maybe you'll gain six months.

They say with Simazine and Dylox
you might boost your profits,
though they don't say what the chemicals cost.

They don't say you might lose a fox
or a cow, a crow or a child.
They don't say you might murder a river
or rub out a meadow.
They just say time is money,
and money's the star on top.

■ POWER LINE
ANDREW WREGGITT

Slashing trees for the power line
a knife-cut through brush
A new geometry
violent as steel to flesh
as blade to frozen wood
He bangs mittened hands together
waiting for a sensation of pain
then starts his saw
Wood chips bleat out
from the base of the tree
The vibration
begins to numb his body again

The graveyard of winter
yields in hard-fought inches
Cold weeks lie ahead

static on the hills
stretching for miles

In the pickup
two men sit
with hard hats
clothes steaming in the warm
gasoline smell of the truck
He works, waiting for his turn
to warm hands, have a smoke
adjust clothing
The monotony of days measured
by the cycle
of turns in the truck
lunch time, quitting time
No one thinks in terms of miles

■ SLOW LEARNER
BRUCE HUNTER

1

the way the kid told me
working for the summer
hometown Standard, Alberta
your basic five elevator
one drugstore no bar town
on a spur line near Drumheller
town foreman got him pruning poplar
gave him enough work
to keep out of trouble
the three days he was gonna be gone
prune em up good, top em off here
pointing somewhere near his belt
three days later the foreman was back
all over town, not a tree
higher than the belt on his pants

2

this winter the kid's working on my crew
we're pruning young cottonwood
which stand about chest high
each tree's got two main stems

51

might look like two
if you didn't know

he's down on the other end
when i decide to see how he's doing
he's gone and cut down every second stem
figuring the other one was a sucker

we kick snow over the stumps
cut down the other half
so the boss won't ever figure
there was a tree here

for the sake of history i'm hoping
we'll both be gone before the snow

■ CHILL FACTOR
BRUCE HUNTER

sun is a white marble eye
sunk in a scowl of cloud
February high in the trees
with chain saw and pole pruners
the union's red book says
at -20 i can pull my crew off the job
this once the boss goes by the book

what isn't said
is that -15 with a light wind
it's thirty below by any chill factor
the steel floor of the cherry picker
under the thick soles of my boots
white hot with frost
metal tools cannot be held

the others on the ground
move like arctic monsters
their faces stiff red masks
curse me, this nether state and the mother
who brought them to this cold place
at the sight of the boss's jeep
running so warm

snow has melted off the roof
his sports jacket open at the neck
he calls me down
to crack about Santa Claus
and the frost on my beard

if the pay wasn't good
winter work less scarce
his skull would be a snowball
in the fist of my anger
instead, courtesy of the crew
a snag of poplar near-misses
covering the windshield with deadfall
a warning that ensures
he won't be back for days

■ TREEPLANTING IN THE RAIN
JIM DODGE

Once you're soaked
it doesn't matter
if it's raining.

The trees go in,
one by one by one,
and you go on

borne and lost in
that mindless rhythm,
bent to the work.

No time at all,
you forget the rain,
blur into its

monotony.
Between root and breath
no difference:

it's all hard work.
Your wet body burns
from the bones out.

■ CONVOY
Tim McNulty

the close-spaced truck
headlights
the long line
climbing the valley road
at dawn
looked
like some old war movie
& us
camped high on the ridge
in our trucks
& smokestacks
could have been
a guerrilla band
but
for the fact that
the cover of trees
was conspicuously
absent
and we were working for the bastards

■ THE COOKSWEAT AND THE MECHANIC
Dymphny Koenig-Clement

for "Monty" LaMontagne

Let me buy you a beer,
he grins, passing
one gone warm and flat
in the kiln of his tent.
We slouch in the dust
and wavering cookshack heat,
sucking back brew.

Outside, in pathetic heaps
lie a broken van
and a dead trike.
Resurrection
is up to him,
he of the bloody knuckles,
the good-natured curses,

who with the wrong tools
and non-existent parts
keeps us mobile.

Inside, the ovens
take the heat higher
while I fight a losing
battle with flies
and stove space.
Revitalization
is up to me.
I feed them the
illusion of contentment,
fill bellies to ward off
any ache and pain.

In this scorched dustbowl
where even the wind burns,
we chuckle at each other's sweat
and frustrations,
holding tight to a
ten minute respite
stolen from ourselves.
On either side crowd
Panic and Pressure,
like demanding parents,
awakening Guilt,
our archenemy.

But this banter
erases the frown from my face,
this laughter is
more precious than gold;
and from our warm embrace
we both draw the strength
to go on.

■ RECURRING NIGHTMARES
DYMPHNY KOENIG-CLEMENT

The aisles of cans
trail into a distant point.

Noname yellow, Campbell soup red.
Colours, names, bargains
in a dizzying pattern.
I remember now that
parallel lines never meet.

My list is three pages long,
closely scribbled hieroglyphics
they can't understand.
Who up north has heard of
tofu, alfalfa sprouts or
any peanut butter other than Kraft?
Six cases of oranges
twelve cases of juice
seventy loaves of bread!
Whole wheat? What's that?
The check-out girl turns white
as my 8, 10, now 12
shopping carts approach.
Must have a pretty big family
little lady, the manager chortles.
Yeah, I want to answer
35 great, big, spoiled brats.

Now the dream shifts,
and I am in the foodstash,
sorting bins of produce,
cleaning good out of the bad.
The tarp-covered pit
has become a sauna,
wilting celery, rotting squash.
There are more slugs in the
case of spinach than leaves,
and in the river
a bucket full of bacon bobs
attracting flies, badgers and bears.

I wake up in a
quiet, West Kootenay night.
It is only February.
All this has yet
to begin.
Again.

■ MADONNA
Dymphny Koenig-Clement

When they see me,
their centre
(not by arrogance
– not by choice)
I smile.
For two hours every morning
and five hours every night
I smile,
calm, friendly, plastic.

When they see me
everything is organized.
Terror shoved in the oven;
panic stuffed in a pot;
crumbs of despair
wiped off an immaculate counter.

When they see me,
I seem to have endless patience
for all their problems,
        their confessions:
each thinks they are unique.
I have a band-aid for a cut,
moleskins for a blister,
backrub for a headache,
hug for a heartache.

When they see me,
I am "Cookie,"
wet-nurse,
shrink,
referee.
I am the one to envy,
well-paid with such
an "easy" job, "stay dry"
"work a few hours a day" . . . .
When they see me.
What they don't see
is the struggle for

four hours sleep a night;
the impersonal alarm
screaming long before theirs;
the aching legs that
can no longer stretch;
the countless water buckets
dragged from the river;
the loneliness; the endless
counting, skimping, balancing;
the mountains of dishes;
the tired circle from counter
to stove to foodstash to
counter to stove –
never seeing sunlight,
never sitting down.

This is what they don't see:
their friendly madonna
crying into the soup,
slaughtering ground beef
in a vengeful rage
against stupidity, or fate.
This is what they don't see,
my pride being tied behind
the starched white apron,
and greed shackling me
to the stove
with green paper chains.
This is what doesn't show.

Chapleau, Ontario

■ PLANTING TODAY IN AFTERNOON HEAT
ROBERT MacLEAN

Planting today in afternoon heat how curious to poke my head
down a deep cool well halfsmothered by the smell wintermint
raspberry alder roots that rough basement. Up again into the
light dipping shy giraffe. Monk of the shovel, I no longer know
how to make any motion except down. Behind me seedlings
stretch a green ribbon to trace my way back to some provisional
home: in front only slash.

I dream 8 x 8. Midseason fugue: tendonitis, muscles twitch,

sucked eyes, silviculture blues. Only a few hardcore tree-junkies remain, taut drained faces. The days elongate, condensing the night, birds singing at 11 p.m., mind infused in insomnia and light. Aurora borealis crackles, the swish of stars. I wake in a cold sweat, hands clenched around a phosphorescent shovel, barely able to shift my neck side to side. Time turns in my belly like a blind man with no hands

▐ TODAY A WASP CRAWLED INTO MY BELLYBUTTON
ROBERT MACLEAN

Today a wasp crawled into my bellybutton. Was he looking for home? Yesterday I inhaled a black fly: it stuck in my sinuses and buzzed like a chainsaw. My ears throb hot and swollen from mosquito bites no-see-ums deer flies with pinto wings albino flies shit flies horseflies who tear out chunks of flesh and go off in the trees to gnaw. Caterpillars nest in my hair, spiders hitchhike on my shoulders, meadowmice tunnel beneath the tent all night partying. Sometimes when I open my mouth to speak invisible winged creatures fly in, causing words to choke. It seems I'm becoming a menagerie, a (sinking) Ark with faces at each porthole. *Open your arms and the earth will breathe you*, a sparrow cheeps as he falls

▐ ON MY TENTH ANNIVERSARY AS A TREEPLANTER
FINN WILCOX

Nearly a million trees older now
I remember when my children
Were shorter than me
And the hair on my head was
Thick as a stand of doghair hemlock.
No regrets though,
The friends that I love
Still work by my side.
But sometimes,
On cold rainy nights,
These stubborn knuckles
Click and hesitate
When I set down the wine.

■ DIRT WORK
Stephen Lewandowski

Make sure your spade's sharp.
Move from the hip & shoulder,
dip with the spade, thrust, lift
and carry off loose dirt, pivot
and release the load in a wheelbarrow.

My coat is stiff and cold with rain.
Inside I sweat and chafe
against a damp cotton shirt.
The regular contained gestures
remind me of a Copland ballet,
except, instead of style, each
effort brings me a clod of dirt and
splinters from the spade handle.
I back off for a running start,
straining against the full barrow
and hill's incline toward
even, turned-over ground.

I dump it where the garden's planned:
soil to grow flowers and vegetables.
My muscles feel the earth fall
to waiting earth as if it fell
from an unknown part of me.

■ THEY DREAM OF BEING GARDENERS
Bruce Hunter

Among smoking piles of leaves
the gardeners stash straw and pig manure
around the roses to overwinter.
On the curbside, gutted flowers
are forked onto the truck.
Leaves rattle down my neck,
acorns poke my knees,
as boxfuls of tulips, crocuses
are placed into the forked-over soil
with the heels of the hands.

Bone meal dust lifts into the eyes, the nose.
Everywhere burned and broken bone
poured around each bulb.

The gravediggers talk of the stench
of death, when a body is exhumed.
The backhoe cutting through the watertable
unleashes the backwash of graves uphill
and an unholy mist rises from the pit.
A smell that remains for days
in the windless hollow of the cemetery,
on the clothing, in the nostrils.

With each bulb, the burial of some animal part.
The nostrils turn with the stomach.
The smell of smoke and bone.

The other gardeners see themselves
as better than the gravediggers,
who must leave their coveralls
outside the lunchroom,
whose wives will not have them
on those days when the old graves are opened.

But none of them dares look
into the mouths of the graves
just as the gravediggers do not touch the roses.

And the gravediggers dream of being gardeners
having filled too many holes with the dead.
The reminder always too much,
their eyes like plumb bobs
on the surface of this life,
plummet with every shovelful
into the stinking water of the swimmers
in the lake under our feet.

■ BILLY NO LONGER THE KID
Bruce Hunter

mean and mouthy
tough man on the cemetery crew

going for low
but the dead and those nearly
the old guys don't care

at twenty
proud of the fact
he's hot shit on the backhoe
(you can tell by the way he wears his hat
CAT diesel, high off his forehead)

neck red with more than sun
under the striped tank top
gut already roly
from too many lunchroom beers
at the UAW hall

the other day
one tree in the entire place
he hits it in third gear
it takes two trucks
to pull the bucket from the trunk

Billy hatless
broken glasses and nose bloodied
old Carlos tells him
what he already knows
what's the hurry
you're gonna get here soon enough

■ TIRESIAS II
HOWARD WHITE

That must be really Interesting, doing the garbage dump
they say. I try to think how.
They tell me I ought to find interesting stuff.
They ask me if I can read the garbage like Christie Logan
Seem to expect me to make prophecies about our civilization
I think over the stuff I see up there.
For a catskinner used to ploughing
the clean and trackless wastes of the north
it is interesting to find Tampax
jammed into the track-adjuster hole

panty-hose wound around the sprockets
bank records impacted into the belly-pan
it is interesting to realize a healthy HD7-G
can stall dead out trying to move a heap
of used Pampers the size of the Community Hall
it is interesting that most people don't seem to care
what the dump guy knows about the bad condition
of their underwear or Mastercharge account
while others compulsively set fire
to everything even their dogfood cans
causing the whole dump to flare up
in a pillar of orange and turquoise smoke
that towers over the town like a mushroom cloud
filling the local paper with irate letters
and causing me to be hauled on the carpet to face dumb
dump questions I can't answer
because breathing the virulent fumes
has reduced my voice to a reedy squeak for over a week
it is interesting when the whole five-acre lump
begins to glow like plutonium
and the town's weekly by-product
of screwtop wine jugs begins to explode
with dull artillery thuds
ripping up through the ground like Titan missiles
and a forty-pounder of Sommet Rouge
smokes past my ear to splash
against the guard behind my unprotected head
giving me brief intimations of morality –
maybe that's the sort of thing they're looking for.
I have kept my eye open for the dead babies
blackened in the sun finding none
but once there were three bloated sheep, shot in the heads
someone's back-to-the-land project over with a vengeance
and for prophecy it did occur as the Pampers
balled up before me the size of a barn
there could be another population explosion on the way
this was a year before the sociologists
came out with the same news on TV
But don't you get some sort of vision
of society's underbelly? You're an archaeologist of the present
can't you describe us by our leavings
they say. I tell them about the lack of anything old

everything people throw out was new last year
broken-backed sofas the price and size of a compact car
tinselly fabric still gleaming in the sooty firelight
plus carpet smelling of dog more fridges
and automatic washers and electric hot water tanks
than stones in a field masses of plastic
kindergarten lunchbuckets decorated with last year's TV hit
kitchen gizmos briefly made indispensable by a K-Tel ad
toy bulldozers designed by someone who clearly never saw
    one
all the inventive genius of America come to rest
in a single heap of anonymous red yellow blue
it is a long, depressing list that adds up, in the end,
to very little
my admirers tend to frown and change the topic
but then us prophets are used to that

■ **WEST COAST**
Zoë Landale

for Howie White

These fishermen, come spring
they pack everything
aboard
but their soft emotions.
Paper towel, rum & hooks
winter-time strategies,
logbooks;
patient details of years.
Survival suits, to forestall
hypothermia.
Ketchup.

Boat by boat, the fleet
splinters from land,
closing universes.
At sea, elections
& earthquakes pass unnoticed.
Revolutions
are known only as
headlines
encountered in ancient newspapers

while painting.
Insulated
& comforted with ocean,
fishermen dream of
little;
fish, fragments of worry
about weather,
a smoking generator.

Packed away like photographs,
wives & children lie
one-dimensional
in drawers.
Every week or so, while
searching for something else,
fishermen will uncover their
images.
Some will phone home.
Others will shrug: *families*,
only able to recall
vague regret
as for an ancient aunt, who
died the other year.

 ### THE 1982 PURSE SEINE ROE HERRING FISHERY
(Northern Area)
M.C. WARRIOR

attention the purse seine roe herring fleet!
this is the Fisheries Patrol Vessel Fence Post!
an announcement
concerning a possible opening
in Kitkatla will be made
in one half hour.

one hundred thousand horses
steam north.
attention the roe herring purse seine fleet!
this is the Fisheries Patrol Vessel Com Post!
an announcement
concerning a possible opening
in Stryker Bay will be made

in one half hour.

one hundred thousand horses
steam south.

attention the purse seine roe herring fleet!
this is the Fisheries Patrol Vessel Last Post!
an announcement
concerning a possible opening
in Cumshewa will be made
in five minutes.

one hundred thousand horses
foam northwest.

two hundred motorized
vessels of wrath seeking
to vent on hapless fish
their long month's frustration.

        meanwhile, in Cumshewa Inlet
        the herring school, seeking relief
        from their long year of celibacy
        and a private place
        where among the kelps
        they may embrace.

but on the surface, in the air,
sounders and sonars, Cessnas
and helicopters, a whole host
of electronic voyeurs
are lurking, hoping
to cause a massive
coitus interruptus.

a flock of vultures circling,
a pack of wolves loping
across the northern Pacific,
waiting for the word
which will spill
a flood of skiffmen
from bunks and galleys,

and a river of nets
over a hundred sterns.

klaxons shatter eardrums.
searchlights flicker and probe
each pore of the coast.
deer flee panic stricken
from screams of "stand by!"
and two hundred diesels
begin to whine like Stukas
hungry for cities.

against us who can prevail?
from hundreds of millions of dollars
worth of steel and technology
who can hide?

but at daybreak
the shoreline
is white with spawn.
and as the news
filters into Steveston
our creditors turn
white with shock.

the purse seine roe herring fleet
      has skunked again.

■ DEEP LINING
CAROLYN BORSMAN

> Despair works from the inside
> at the guts, the bellows,
> like sea lice swarming.
>
> Waiting for halibut
> in the cutting rain,
> we pull dogfish up
> one after another.
>
> On the seventh day
> rasping on the line,

another fish offers itself,
another belly dances
like a white rag,
parasites spilling out the holes.

Some truce.
A fish hooked on the bottom
too long is eaten alive.

Young Stuart hits the lousy dogs
with a club back into the sea;
John, his cold eyes blasted
by the wind
screams over the edge, "Sonofabitch
whore suckers!"
Jerry mutters the mothers
are eating his heart out.

Inside me, the indignity goes deeper.
I know the bottom line
and still, I rise to the bait.

Down go the buoy and the marker, the fathoms of rope
and the anchor, and along the sea bed a thousand or two
of line, with hooks and bait like the backbone of
a poisonous fish. Another anchor, so many fathoms,
then a buoy and flag.

We call it a set, and wait to pick up again on a great
winch. Sea cucumbers, skate, sole, rat fish, dog fish,
cod, red snappers, sea bass --with the skipper up top
in the wheelhouse swearing "halibut" until there is one.

It comes like a brown tarpaulin of kelp to green water.
Two hundred pounds, two bullets from a rifle, three
long gaffs. This fish can break a man's leg with the slap
of its tail. Halibut fights for space to hover free,
with no light piercing its tiny brain.

■ HALIBUT
Douglas Dobyns

There's a rescue going on a couple of miles west of us – we
can see the Coast Guard circling around and the skipper's in
there on the radio while minutes are ticking down toward the
noon closure. Weather's up and the halibut are just flying
on board – we're in a pile of them now so high that some
are flopping back over and I'm pitching them down the hatch
as fast as I can put a gaff on 'em.

Time's up and the skipper yells to cut it but the other deck
hand's up on the boom now and yelling to just keep pulling
while he watches for the plane – we're pulling close to a
hundred pounds a minute now and the boat's gonna get
    plugged
soon at this rate.

Weather is snotty and that's good for what we're about –
probably two skates left and only one of them will deck-load
this little pisspot. If only we hadn't been crossed by that
stuck gear! This line would be on and we'd be gone.

But the skipper's paranoid and he's going to cut it himself
laughing that goofy laugh and now it's done. We have a lot
of shit to tie down now to get this load back under cover of
land and it's gonna be a buck all the way in for 70 cold miles.

The boat's got a load on for these conditions and that's a fact
but the deckies are greedy – you only get 24 hours and you
only get on the fish like this once even if you're lucky. So
the tag end is flopping toward the bottom now with another
grand apiece clipped between that cut and the anchor.

We'll do okay with what we have so now it's time to clean up
this mess and ease in for shore as the wind comes up. And
comes up. And when the fish are down and you've stood watch
you wedge yourself in somewhere and sleep in spite of the
crazy dangerous pounding of this upsidedown worked-out world.

■ SEPPO
CAROLYN BORSMAN

Palm open,
fog passes a cool and tender hand
over the small faces
of a trawling fleet.
Boats slip side to side,
wires pull in rhythm.

A radar hums
a song for blindness.

Birds fly to sea
when fog reaches land.
Lost, some fall between white fingers,
the cross of bow poles
and rigging strung like web.

A fisherman stands watchful
in the stern,
his thick glasses cluttered with dew.
He wipes them clean.

Twenty miles at sea
a bird drops, exhausted.

> Onto a button
> at the top of his white cap
> it falls.

> The skipper holds his head
> afloat while the bird sleeps.

> Neither move for the wild flight
> of fish on the line
> > that darts from its own blood
> > > beating down.

> His hands still,
> Seppo smiles, until
> what seems years,

the bird lights onto his shoulder,
to the deck,
head poised –

I hear the strike of the bell.
Though time has passed
and blinded me,
Seppo is here.

■ VANCOUVER HARBOUR
CAROLYN BORSMAN

Bell buoys sound in a wake
for the dead and the busy
as debris rolls in, punk boats
in the lick of trawlers, seiners,
sailboats.
Shoals whisper along Spanish Banks
speaking traffic in the spill of trade.
Freighters at anchor, silhouettes,
rise black. Tugs crossing
red white white green lit stacks
sweep across,   long shadows in tow.

Two a.m., tides change, music stations
play in the wires, car doors slam,
the oil drum sound of the engine,
city bound, slows.

As the commerce of the living slips
through Lions Gate Narrows,
our engine near standstill in green light,
silence concentrated as yellow sulphur
pouring from blue chutes,
bridge lights blinking,
a sudden back-flow of beauty swirls
through the clutch of motors,
and oil weeps quietly into the night.

■ THE FISHERMAN AND THE LOGGER
Howard White

You can spot a fisherman anywhere.
There is a roll to his walk.
There is a mournful whine in his voice,
sharpened by years of complaining about bad catches.
There's a sadness, a slowness, as if
too deep knowledge of the darkness below life's surfaces
had taken the hurry out of him. A patience
born of waiting – waiting for weather and tide
waiting for the fish to appear.
No one learns more of waiting than the fisherman.

In the fisherman's eye is none of the animal spark
you find in the logger's eyes, no scent
of male animal, twitching tail. Fishing
isn't so dumbly masculine a species of work as logging –
women take well to its slow but intricate rhythm.

The logger is up in the pub bothering the barmaids
and starting fights; the fisherman is down on the dock
sitting on a fish box jawing politics and mending gear.
The logger has a new tinsel shirt he will tell you
how outrageously he paid for, but it will
be on the floor, once used and ruined when he leaves.
The fisherman has on wool and tweeds bagged to his shape
and prefers to drink on the boat among his own.

In the eye of the fisherman is a diffuse deepness
like the cloudy gulf he lets his gear into,
and his mind. The logger's work is fast and dangerous;
he must keep his eyes wide open.

The fisherman works blind, feeling
his familiar but never-known world
with the sightless, superstitious part of the mind.

The logger is strong, like the land
but the fisherman is stronger

like the sea.

SOMETHING THEY CLAIM CAN'T BE MADE
Women Working

■ FIRST DAY ON A NEW JOBSITE

SUSAN EISENBERG

Never again a first day like the
First Day
            that Very First one,
when only the sternest vigilance
kept the right foot following the left
following the right following the left,
each step a decision, a victory of
willpower over fear, future over past.
Margaret's out there / Keep going /
She's been working a few
weeks already / She's managing/
Keep going / The legs buck
LA / Seattle / Detroit / women passing
through construction site gates for the
first time / Keep going / Right following
Go home if you want! / But
tomorrow / What'll you do for work
tomorrow? / left following right up to
the gate
            where a man hands me hard hat and
goggles and points me toward a trailer
where the conversation
                        stops
                        as I enter:
Well, what'll we talk about now.
Can't talk about girls.

And then Ronnie, the one with beady eyes
and a gimp leg, who knows for a fact –
            one of the girl apprentices
            is a stripper in the Zone –
says to my partner
                        Give me your apprentice
and I follow him, tripping over cinder blocks,
to a small room
                        where he points to the ceiling:
I need some hangers 11 inches off the ceiling /
Here's the Hilti /
The rod and strut are in the corner /

75

The ceiling's marked where I want
holes drilled and leaves
                              without
                    explaining
                              hanger
                              rod
                              strut
or seeing that the bit on the heavy drill
barely reaches
                    the x-marks on the ceiling
when I stand tiptoe on the ladder's
                                        top step.

                    ■

Knowing which words to use
          what jokes to banter
          how to glide the body through dangers
                    without knocking anything
                              or anyone;
learning to speak first
          and define the territory
                    of conversation.
Passing.

                    ■

Another
          first day: the job new
the workers all strangers, all men
myself   the only 'female'
                              and yet
we find, almost easily, the language
that is common:
          Get me some 4-inch squares
                    with three-quarter k-o's —
          Need any couplings or connectors?
          No, but grab some clips and c-clamps
                    and some half-inch quarter-twenties.
Passwords.
          You know what you're doing in a panel?
          Sure.

Mechanic to mechanic.

76

Never again a first day like the
First Day.

■ THROUGH THE CEILING, MAIDEN VOYAGE
SUSAN EISENBERG

Sliding
        under an airduct, then
scrabbling crab-like along pipes and crossbars –
    my flashlight breaking
    the darkness, my bodyweight
    placed gingerly (not to fall through) –

I ask the stillness,
has another woman passed
                        before me?
to witness this
            pulsation of buildinglife:

arteries of plumbing pipes branch across
electric nervelines   sinews of metal
secure airducts
            pumping coolbreath / warmbreath
                    to the skeletal
framework of iron beams.

How many times I have passed
under ceilings
            unaware
                    unsuspecting.

■ 'GIRL' ON THE CREW
KATE BRAID

The boys flap heavy leather aprons at me
like housewives scaring crows
from the clean back wash.
        Some aprons.   Some wash.
They think if the leather is tough enough
if the hammer handle piercing it is long enough
I will be overcome with primordial dread
or longing.

77

They chant construction curses at me:
        Lay 'er down! Erect those studs!
and are alarmed when I learn the words.
They build finely tuned traps, give orders I cannot fill
then puzzle when a few of their own
give me pass words.

I learn the signs of entry,
dropping my hammer into its familiar mouth
as my apron whispers O-o-o-h Welcome!

I point my finger and corner posts spring into place
shivering themselves into fertile earth at my command.
The surveyors have never seen such accuracy.

I bite off nails with my teeth
shorten boards with a wave of my hand
pierce them   through the dark brown love knots.
They gasp.

I squat and the flood of my urine digs whole drainage systems
in an instant.
The boys park their backhoes, call their friends
to come see for themselves or they'd never believe it.

The hairs of my head leap to steel and join boards,
        tongue-in-groove
like lovers along dark lanes.
Drywall is rustling under cover
eager to slip over the studs at my desire.

When I tire, my breasts grow two cherry trees
that depart my chest
and offer me shade, cool juices
while the others suck bitter beans.

At the end of the day the boys are exhausted
from watching.
They fall at my feet and beg for a body like mine.
I am too busy dancing to notice.

■ THESE HIPS
KATE BRAID

For Me To Read

Some hips are made for bearing
children, built like stools
square and easy, right
for the passage of birth.

Others are built like mine.
A child's head might never pass
but load me up with two-by-fours
and watch me
bear.

When the men carry sacks of concrete
they hold them high, like boys.
I bear mine low, like a girl
on small, strong hips
built for the birth
of buildings.

■ HANGING IN, SOLO
(So What's It Like To Be The Only Female On The Job?)
SUSAN EISENBERG

On the sunshine rainbow days
womanhood
clothes me in a fuchsia velour jumpsuit and
crowns me with a diamond hardhat.
I flare my peacock feathers
and fly through the day's work.
                    Trombones sizzle
as my drill glides through cement walls
                    through steel beams.
Bundles of pipe rise through the air
at the tilt
        of my thumb.
Everything I do
            is perfect.

The female of the species
advances 10 spaces and
takes an extra turn.

On the mudcold-grey-no-
sun-in-a-week days womanhood
weighs me down in colourless arctic fatigues;
hands me an empty survival kit;
and binds my head in an iron hardhat
                three sizes too small.
I burrow myself mole-like into my work, but
my tampax leaks;
my diamond-tip bit burns out after one hole;
my offsets are backwards;
all of my measurements are wrong.
At each mistake, a shrill siren
alerts all tradesmen on the job
                to come laugh at me.
Everything I do
                must be redone.

The female of the species
loses her next turn
and picks a penalty card.

On most days, those
partly sunny days that bridge the
rainbow sunshine days and the mudcold-
grey days
                womanhood outfits me in a
flannel shirt and jeans
and hands me a hardhat just like
everyone else's. I go about my work like
a giraffe foraging the high branches:
stretching myself comfortably.
As I hang lighting fixtures and make splices,
I sing to myself
                and tell myself stories.
Everything I do
                is competent enough.

The female of the species
advances 1 space
and awaits her next turn.

■ THEY SAID WOMEN ALWAYS QUIT
DONNA LANGSTON

We were hired at the same time.
Some of the first women out on oil refinery crews.
We made it through training, climbing towers,
putting out fires, crawling up slippery pipe
racks, learning to tolerate the taste of beer –
at 6 a.m. after night shift, and tryin, tryin,
tryin to be friends with "the boys."

Our slip-ups, unlike theirs, were logged in
memories, stories, legend.
No matter how we dressed, we were provocative.
In summer our jeans and cotton shirts were
provocative.
In winter our jeans and rainboots were provocative.

The night you went home doubled in pain from
complications with sterilization surgery, they all
talked about how a woman couldn't work this job.

The night I called in sick during a snowstorm
cause my son was delirious with fever, they said
we couldn't stand the weather.
They placed bets that we wouldn't last.

One night you came into work
after a two day absence
with a black eye.
You told everyone but me
that you'd run into a door.

After you and your husband split
you tried to keep working shift work
as a single parent with five kids.
When you had to quit you cried cause you knew

you'd be back on welfare and they said
women always quit.

After you'd left, I heard of a man at the plant
whose wife died two years earlier
and left him a single parent with one child.
"The boys" started a petition and got him on
straight day shift so he could take care of his
daughter.

I walked to our hangout, the bathroom,
the night I heard that,
looked at myself in the mirror
and cause you weren't there to say it,
in a strong whisper I told myself,
"Hang in there – show them – you can do it."

■ FACTORY GIRLS
JONI MILLER

dot's worked here 20 years
and she smiles at you
in the morning
jenny meant to be a model
but her face broke out
laurane wants to train
to be an adjuster
"that's a man's job" they told her
and all the men
walked out of the plant
in protest
still norma clutches her union card
the only hope she has
"why do you work here?"
gracie asked us.

■ THE WOMEN'S COMMITTEE
LEONA GOM

two men come to our meeting,
they are only middle-management,
but still we are delighted, whisper

to each other, *at last*
they are taking us seriously.
our fingers gush with reports
and statistics. we eat up
their advice, they tell us
what we are doing wrong.
at coffee break we flock to talk
to them, thank them for
coming. our smiles stretch across
our faces like rubber bands, snap
back when they are gone and
nothing is on the table except
papers, the flat hunger
of type.

■ WAITING
Leona Gom

after the meeting the women go to lunch.
the waitress watches, awkward on her high heels
like some odd hoofed animal, while we decide.
a smile is stapled on her face like part
of the menu. small puckers of burns
are splattered part-way up one arm. she is
all of us, our first lurch into the working
world, learning to sell service, it is
where we begin, before we become
the women who go to meetings, the ones
who are never satisfied, we are pains
in the management ass, we're as tired of it
as they are, but still we keep asking,
saying, 64% is not enough, the waitress
is still who we are, coins rattle
their judgments in her pocket.
when she brings us our bill she asks
is there anything more that we want.

■ QUILTING BEE
Sandy Shreve

So this is it, the female
job ghetto. Seems

to be a lot of us here

our cheeks crinkling into
weathered grins, fingers
pecking at paper, eyes
at the air

Days and nights
                    fragmented
                    as if
we were collecting shreds
of time
for a fabulous quilt.

Well, perhaps we are

Might just one day
sew it up into something

they claim can't be made

■ CAVITIES
LEONA GOM

> *If there is no face in the mirror, marry.*
> *If there is no shadow on the ground,*
> *have a child. These are the conventions*
> *the will consents to. But there is a face.*
> *There is a shadow. They are simply*
> *unsuitable.*
> ■ Jane Rule, *Desert of the Heart*

sometimes I have a daughter.
she is 15 now, I worry
about her friends, is she taking drugs.
but I raised her well, I am sure of that,
I am a mother, it is
my name.

sometimes I have a daughter,
when I am alone in my office
at night, off-guard, a headache
a crack across my temples, the day's

84

perspiration hardening like wax into
my pores, my briefcase swollen
with work. she is the choice I think
would have saved me
from being here now, my life full
the way a file cabinet is full,
the way a tooth is filled
but ticking still with that faint pain
no pill can work away.

PIECE BY PIECE YOU DELIVER YOURSELF
Service Work

ADJUSTMENT 1:
Shifting Piles
LESLÉA NEWMAN

I place a pile of credits to my left
and a pile of debits to my right.
After I type the numbers from the debits
onto the credits
I pile the debits on top of the credits.
Then I pull the carbons from the credits
and separate the copies into piles.
I interfile the piles
and bring them over to the files
where I file the piles and pull the files
making a new file of piles.
Then I make files
for the pile that had no files
and put them into a new file pile.
I take the new file pile
down the aisle
over to the table where Mabel
makes labels for April to staple.
I take the new labelled stapled file pile
back down the aisle over to the file
to be interfiled with the pile of filed files.
After I file April's piles
I get new debits from Debby
and new credits from Kerry.
I carry Kerry's credits and Debby's debits
back to my desk
and place a pile of credits to my left
and a pile of debits to my right.
After I type the numbers from the debits
onto the credits
it's 10:00
and we have exactly fifteen minutes
to go down to the cafeteria
and drink coffee
or go out into the parking lot
and scream.

■ SECRETARY 1
MICKEY BICKERSTAFF

She is training another new boss
(her third in ten years).
Like a mother with a sick child,
she cheerfully passes up lunch
to nurse him through
the hesitant first weeks of
what-do-we-do-with-this?

Soon, he will banish her
back into her bottle of Liquid Paper,
like Cinderella's godmother, or a genie
who has outlived her wishes
(another fairy tale ending gone astray),
leaving time to settle over her again,
like dust on a forgotten ornament.

■ MEDITATION ON A TYPO
CATHERINE SHAW

Only a moment ago there was flux
and a gladness of speed –
the ribbon flying in its gears,
the paper blooming, a blur of ink,
the keys tapping smartly
like a dozen pairs of heels.

Yes my fingers flitted like moths
over the keys, doing their dance,
their daily word dance.
Once learned, it is a skill natural as talk.
And yet, there are always the obstacles.
Always, as with the tongue, the telling slips.
The fingers slide or drag or disobey.
The mechanism fails.

> And so, I have done it again.
> Made a wordclot.
> Botched the language.
> Goofed.

The ragged thing is grinning at me stupidly.
It looks diseased, like bad teeth.
It is, in its own way, monstrous:
a word without a breath of meaning,
its consonants colliding like the blind.

As always, I will do my best to fix it –
dabbing on the white fluid as if it were iodine,
then blowing on the page as if it were burned.
Soon, I'll be typing again –
first over the scar
and then into new untried territory,
grateful for a second chance,
hoping to heaven no one notices
the shadow on the back side of the page.

■ RESIGNATION
CATHERINE SHAW

This, superiors,
is to offer you
my resignation.
Too many years have passed
without recompense
and without sentience
too many days,
each one vacant
as the bare vestibule
I pass through
day after hollow day
from or to
the circle of sorry labour
I inhabit
that is my habit,
my subordination.

Automaton, I
go about my work
in mindless quietude,
totting up numbers,
filling out forms,
stacking and stapling –

so efficient! –
but watching every minute
on your grey clock
loiter and drag
on its tired trail
to the tired end of day.

And what of
those dear others
who share my circle
and whose faces match
my own encrypted face?
They are not dear.
Away from here,
they live lives
I can't imagine
in small and singular worlds
that have no use for me.
If there's friendship here,
it's made of shallow stuff,
of pleasantries,
enforced equivalence:

the accident of company!

I soon learned
to be on guard against
such amity,
to cultivate
the ingrown point-of-view,
pruning away
those shoots of anger
and intelligence
that would expose to me
the baseness
of your hierarchy.
It's just as well.
I may be dwarfed
but how much worse
to flare up
in my insignificance
and be unheard

and change nothing
and destroy only me.

"I will seek work elsewhere!"
That has been my quest:
a foolish enterprise,
a grail of styrofoam at best.
Wherever I go,
I find your duplicate:
vestibule, paperwork,
watched clocks
and grey-eyed vacancy.
What's the good of going?
I'm too weary now
to take my future in my hands
and forge another way.
This, superiors,
is to offer you my resignation.
I'll stay.

■ **SECRETARY**
MIRIAM GOODMAN

Her desk creates a harbour in the hall.
Without a cubicle to hide in, she's approachable
like land on the horizon. Close in,
you see her swivel round, serene, her finger-
nail on HOLD, pale and polished
at the black Selectric.
A bud vase with a rose he gave her.
Every day she brings the lunch her mother packs.

Against the waves of new disorder
she hurls the force of her restraint,
a bulwark when you come at her:
"Have we more envelopes like this one?"
She tells twice like a channel buoy, sounding
a firm *keep off*: "No, we don't, Miriam.
We have none at the present time.
They've been on order since July."
Her answer keeps you right on course.

■ XEROX
Miriam Goodman

White page
green bar of light
crossing the miles of the page
like an iron

comes to the end
goes out
don't bring it up again
don't bring it up

apron of light
pertinent, topical,
ON and levitating
works till 5

On the highway,
steady moon,
blinking arrows
here, then blank

turn signals
throbbing on and off
intermittent
red

doing the same thing all the time
the exact same:
following the lights,
light passing in a slit
below the door.

■ CAFETERIA
Miriam Goodman

Clock up on the wall
eggs us on. We pack
the table for a game
of cards. Electric waxer
works here twice a day

on schedule,
bumping the machines.
In goes a quarter
good as a base hit.
Down falls juice in cans.
Up goes a cheer.
Salt and sugar: free
done up in packets.
Bundled like grains,
we strain at limits.
The machinist who buys coffee
finds me writing, asks
if I am making a report
on the people who buy coffee
in the middle of the afternoon.

■ SANCTUARY
CATHERINE SHAW

A plain place, all tile and porcelain –
airless, with an echoing of heels,
prone to leakage, soiled
in spite of constant disinfecting,
ill-lit, paper-strewn...

But also private, with a row of doors
to dream behind, a row of doors to slam
whenever a slam is necessary.
Near these, a row of sinks
to rinse the taint from our corporate hands.
And how useful the mirrors are,
reflecting a taut chin or a troubled brow,
guiding as we powder them to realignment.

Tears are welcome here, for men are not.
Talk is welcome here, for no one works.
Is it any wonder that we enter here so often,
moved by needs more urgent
than the ones the room was built for?

No, my enviers, peering sidelong
beyond the closing door –

It isn't vanity that draws us to the mirrors
nor filth that calls us to the stalls –
we are here because of the trials of there.
We are here for sanctuary.

■ COMPANION
Sandy Shreve

This machine is advertised
as a companion: personal
computer
or perhaps I misunderstand
and the innuendo implies
status.

Neither interpretation is real:
it takes up space in my office
but it is in fact, mere
mechanical apparatus,
a replacement part in the false
hierarchy of jobs

an absence
of someone else's hands
sharing the full range of work
side-by-side with mine

■ COMPUTER LAB
Miriam Goodman

How do the programmers look when they work?
Some sit for hours and the room is full of noise.
Keyboards clack. Behind concentric grillwork –
whirring fans. Hammers knock the print heads
on the teletypes. And under the assault, the programmers
slide down in the chairs like paper in the platen.
Chins on chests. A desultory finger lifts and strikes
a key. The image on the cathode-ray-tube changes.
Bluish light. The disconnected dots construct a message.
Dry and steady, thought pays out like rope.
They breathe, they shift their weight, they tilt
their heads, they flex their feet. So silent

are the programmers, sitting under torrents
of white noise.

■ DEATH OF A COMPUTER OPERATOR
RICHARD GROSSMAN

Working the graveyard shift he dug
his grave in our tape vault strapping his chin
to the side of a rack:
his knees hung six inches off the ground.

Everybody said he was meticulous
and that he did everything correctly up until the day
he died. His handwriting, according to the Coroner,
was firm.

He worked for us for over a year
turning out massive amounts of information
late at night
but when we called to notify his mother that we cut him
down she said

keep the body.

■ MANUAL ACTION 1*
PAM TRANFIELD

when we arrive in the morning
the computers are up   waiting
the screens are ready   willing
and able to work   they flash:
Good Morning!
The System is Ready!

our job
to explain your UIC claim
over the telephone:
letter and number codes
on the VDTs denote
overpayments   disqualifications
disentitlements;
in turn we must code your questions

disagreements
onto forms called Pinkies:

> Claimant disagrees with D3. Please Advise.
> Cheque sent week code 528-3. Not received. Please Trace.

no room on the Pinkie for:

> Claimant feeding family. Please send cheque today.
> Caller severely depressed. Two weeks left on claim. Caller likely suicidal.
> Overpayment resulted from UIC clerical error. Operator agrees with claimant. System fucked.

*In Unemployment Insurance Commission lingo an MA-1 means contentious claim.

■ HAVE YOU EVER CONSIDERED...
SUSAN MEURER

"Have you ever considered,"
the world famous ophthalmologist asked,
peering at the
>   bloodshot, tearing, aching eyes,
"another type of work?"
My VDT-tortured eyes, twitching again,
begged for a break from green letters
and glare eight hours a day.
White coated doctor-priest had informed me,
there was nothing wrong with my vision.
Of course, no cataracts, glaucoma nor
>   imminent blindness,
>   Just an inability to
>   read in my free time,
>   watch TV with my children,
>   focus on sewing or knitting.
"Yes," I answered, "I've considered
>   airline reservation clerk,
>   customer service rep,
>   telephone operator,
>   draftsman,
>   newspaper reporter,
>   government typist,

medical transcriptionist,
bookkeeper,
programmer.
How about you?"

■ BACK IN THE SHOP
SUSAN MEURER

I'm back in the shop.
One shift – eight hours.
I can turn my thoughts to measurable units:
    Picas, points, ems and ens.
    Bell codes, kerning values, ligatures,
All surface and circle in my mind.
But I'm not sure
I still have the necessary stuff
To do the job:
    The speed, the accuracy, the skill.

I revel in the camaraderie,
The give and take of co-workers.
I remember: that was always
The best reason for going to work every day.
Donna's latest wedding plans,
Rob's progress in night school.
And yes, even the hockey pool –
I won it two weeks in a row
Without knowing who scored
And for which team.
I enjoy a 15-minute coffee break,
A lunch hour, where the food
Each of us unpacks reveals our deepest secrets.
Once again the day is divided
Into discernible parts,
And as the last half hour approaches
My imagination takes me beyond the time clock.

At the end of the shift
I inspect the fruits of my labour:
Tangible, touchable and best of all, immediate.
Neat black and white galleys
Lining the counter,

Most of them free of major disasters,
Each the translation of someone else's ideas
Into the printed word.

What a relief to know
That I still can practice an honest trade
And create wealth,
Even if it includes surplus value.
When this payslip reaches me
I'm absolutely certain how I earned
every penny.

ONCE WHEN I WAS A BANK CLERK
(a work poem for Tom Wayman)
GLEN SORESTAD

Now you see, Tom
when I was seventeen, my uncle was a banker
Well, to be more precise (as poets should) he was
really an accountant in The Canadian Bank of Commerce
and I was a high school graduate with nowhere to go

My teachers said, "Sorestad, your ability tests
and your aptitude tests and your personal preference tests
all clearly indicate that you love the outdoors
you have a flair for language, a hatred for numbers
and a deep desire to be entirely your own man
so why don't you become a nature journalist?"

So, armed with this weight of educational certainty
I joined The Canadian Bank of Commerce

Posted to my first prairie branch in Canora, Saskatchewan
I was as green as any bank trainee could ever be
and was immediately sent on the usual fruitless errands
vets of the bank reserve with glee for rookies
(You see, Tom, bankers have their own versions
of sending the newcomer off to fetch a skyhook
or to exchange this hammer for a left-handed one)
So on my second day the accountant sent me
to the town's only other bank, our competitor
to borrow from them their General Ledger

Off down the street I went, simple as soup
and sauntered into The Royal Bank of Canada
spotted another young guy working behind the counter
and told him my bank needed their General Ledger

Well, it turned out he was a rookie too, so *he got it*
and I wandered out with the huge volume, unnoticed
When I walked back through the bank's front door
it seems all the staff including the manager were gathered
waiting, set to give me the royal raspberries
I remember thinking how odd they looked, Tom
as I lugged in that Ledger like a tablet of stone
and thunked it down on the counter before the accountant
Faces fell, the manager blanched, wheeled into his office
His apologies flew down the street by phone
Without a word the accountant rushed the Ledger back
Seems the General Ledger was sacred in the bank
never to be let out of sight, nor seen by anyone else
but they hadn't bothered to inform my counterpart nor me
so we were the only unembarrassed ones in the incident

Well Tom, after that I'll tell you
they didn't try any more of the usual bank jokes
neither on me, nor on the other lucky rook
I guess they were afraid to even speculate
what we might bring back

■ TECH WRITER
Roger Taus

I'm in livery
to the Bnk
grinding
the dollars
you can't
live
over
to the cent
so Oly & Figueroa
in ell ay
the sidewalk
leadsback to

work
hey whiteboy
gimmie a job
upstairs
it's Vincent's hallway decor
Houses at Auvers
the skies of Provence
a breath of art here
always crazier
@ full moon

■ THE BOOK TRUCK
Sandy Shreve

"I won't support
across-the-board:
librarians deserve
much more than clerks."

And me there squatting
at her feet
on my knees
digging out dingy
volume after volume
from the book truck
stacking them in shelves
so I can clothe them later
with shining covers
bored and sneezing
from the dust
of the dreary back room

"Too bad if you can't
eat well on what you earn."

And my stomach growls
just as hard as hers
for lunch
while I wash books
sort books
stack books
shelve books,

while she sits, pensive
at her desk
reading journals I deliver,
answers questions
patrons ask

I still recall the day
I gave a woman
Atwood's novel
from the shelf where
I was filing books
and she bustled over
yelling: "Never
do that again –
send the borrower to me!"

Even if the book
is in my hand,

she's the librarian
not me:
I shelve books

■ ELM
NICK MUSKA

Elm Storage #3 Warehouse is a
warehouse
a place, a space.
The Mostov Brothers
own it.
Lee and me
work there.

Believe it.
This is not
metaphysics.
We work there.

500,000 square feet
of space
Pennsy RR track

alongside
six freightdoors
to the siding
five loading docks
forklifts.
Trucks, semi's, and
boxcars
to empty
and fill.
Believe it
We work there.

Wall Street one-way
on the front
Ben's Truck Parts junkyard
on our back.
We work there
in between.

There are no elm trees.

■ FORKLIFT POEM / WINTER
NICK MUSKA

for Lew Welch

When I drive lift
  I am saddled to a peeled-paint rhino
  who would charge concrete and crumble block
  If I did not hold it tightly by the ears.

When I drive lift
  I raise three ton with my right hand
  and can tilt, spin, drop it
  like a plumed lead hat.

When I drive lift
  I am the slave of capital, bleeding hydraulic sweat
  and oil in airless semi-trailers, blue-toed
  froze to the gas pedal, gritty.

When I drive lift
  I have a handle on the nuts and bolts of things

pirouetting with iron castings in my jaws
lost without thought.

When I drive lift
   From my rhino perch I am lord of all I survey:
   An iron-dark, echo-empty warehouse
   Ben's junkyard next door, its soil gone oil
   sun glinting hard from stacks of rear-view mirrors.

When I drive lift
   I am the last snorting thing left out on the dock
   breath and exhaust lost in the snowstorm
   blowing under the edge of the overhead doors.

■ WHY IT'S CALLED A WAREHOUSE
Nick Muska

When a customer
calls for a load
we all run around
screaming "Where
is it? Where is it!"

Nobody knows.

■ TWO YEARS
Nick Muska

I keep telling myself I only do this for a living.
My life one busted down railcar after another,
inspection reports, hating the boss always
underfoot saying move two ways at once.
I go home nightly, beat and double-hearted
to lover-wife and lover-lover, doing it
for a living to forget what makes me want
to wake each day grumbling, worrying
over love and I wonder who's kissing them now.
Two years at it now – all water gone under, the
bald Yellow Double T trucker said, pretending
he is Mr. Moto, when I saw the calendars said mid-July
and I remembered sweating out the first day.
I only do this for a living, Jack. I only do this

for a living, Jill. Living is next year
or the next. Or the next.

■ WHAT HAPPENED
Nick Muska

In wintertime, Lee Floyd
was cut twice for hernia.
All spring Lee spit
smoky, goldtooth blood
onto the damp EZ Dri floor.
It happens to the best of us –
A young sculptor I knew
sliding her statues
into better light
and this old black man
hefting 200 lb. tractor tires
into neat six high stacks.
The sculptor healed.

Lee Floyd drew cancer
when they went to cut him
the third time.
Gaiter and I called every day
Heard him go
from critical to critical
to fair to fair
to in and out of
intensive care.
Lost his esophagus
half a stomach
two ribs so they
could get to it
his job
his pension
he don't work here any more.

Gaiter and I
move like estranged lovers
on opposite ends of Elm.
We don't talk much
no jokes on the house phone

We are alone and lonely.
Gaiter smiles once a week
grumbles more than ever
the honeymoon is over.
Our father / brother, Lee
shacked up for this endless winter
with two sisters
in a furlined house.

Sometimes he talks about suing the Teamsters
Fills out forms with me
Hauls pallets for ten bucks
Once a month.
Losing weight
Back on Budweiser
and Pall Malls
Thin, smoky, goldtooth grin
He don't work here any more.

■ FRIENDLY WORLD OF RECEIVING
RONALD KURT

The phone rings
and the ever alert receiver
answers,
"Friendly world of receiving!"
"Ah, yeah,
could you please come down
and carry a microwave out
for a customer?"
"Yes ma'am right away."
Equipped with a trolley
and a positive sense of
direction he arrives to
face a tall and strong
looking young man,
no doubt twice his strength
he figures.
"This could be hard,"
says the tanned young customer
in a deep voice.

"Yeah, it might be,"
answers the receiver as he
grunts under the gaze of this
big guy, lifting and balancing
the microwave on his trolley.
A good mood is gone,
the friendly little receiver
curses his fortune and this
macho man under his breath,
smiles, and asks the customer
the way to his car.

■ PRODUCTIVITY
RONALD KURT

Thanksgiving Day
and we are working,
a skeleton staff
at best now reduced
to two.
Management warns us,
"I want you to concentrate
on productivity,
if I see you guys
doing nothing I'll send
you home."
We mumble f's under
our breath and even figure
on doing nothing,
home sounds like a good
idea,
time and a half however
can't be denied.

■ LAYOFF
RONALD KURT

The layoff is becoming
frightening.
The police departments,
the fire departments,
and sanitation departments

have been hit with major
cutbacks.
"It's getting scary,"
says Al.
"Just think, unloading boxes
used to be despised,
it was for losers,
a job for when you
couldn't get anything else,
already there's been applications
for our department."
"Yeah, the flood has already
begun," says John.
"Soon we'll be looked upon
with envious eyes;
a degree means nothing now-
adays, and even working for
a company for twenty years
doesn't mean your hide's safe."

■ DISPATCHER SAWDUST
KEN RIVARD

it is true,
dispatcher sounds like his voice is cutting wood,
he grinds out orders as if at
any moment someone will pull the plug on him, but
he is a very efficient worker.
he is also the vice-president.
if only the tension would tell him so.

today, I am painting numbers and letters on
a trailer when he comes out
into the yard.
as he begins to speak, a shouting match explodes from
inside the warehouse.
gotta go,
sounds like trouble, he yells.

I climb down from the trailer and follow him inside.
in the crate-making area, I hear
the head warehouseman giving a blast to

a helper for being slow and
the dispatcher tells both men he'll now take over.

carefully, ever so carefully, he begins to cut lumber for
a new crate.
I ask myself if he is using his vocal chords to
fashion the crate.
instead
he uses his nerves,
they are that sharp.

from WHEN THE MOVING COMPANY IS SCHOLARLY: 4
KEN RIVARD

the nervous driver has pills for everything
and when Frankie is assigned to him as his helper
the driver is happy because he doesn't have to teach
and he hates having outside labourers

but today the third man besides Frankie
is outside help
and the driver slips into an ugly mood   they
have to pack and load ten thousand pounds   time
for another pill

on the way to the job the driver tells the outside labourer
his kind are lazy
that all his kind ever do is work just enough
get paid   drink   miss work
and Frankie feels the coming of fists

the outside labourer asks the driver to pull over   climbs
out of the truck
and before slamming the door
the most thought-out middle finger
you could ever imagine
but the driver just grunts   says he
feels better already
and gulps down a yellow capsule

■ MISTAKE
KEN RIVARD

the salesman   very angry with Frankie
about one error in the sales report
and Frankie saying not to worry
as the accounts are not complete
but the salesman is trapped
in his ranting and raving of profits

that night Frankie   thinking of the salesman's temper
and the phone rings   it's him   still steaming
saying he'll tell the president
and Frankie can't believe the irrational noises
throbbing from one ear to the next

Frankie at work   everyone but the president knows
so Frankie stops talking to the salesman
with the hope that his own rage
will scream itself into nowhere

not long afterwards the salesman resigns
tells everyone he's off to medical school
but he only says this
when his eyes are fixed on his desk

a year later someone from the office
walks by that medical school
decides to look up the ex-salesman
but the university has never heard of him
and Frankie finally sees him
not a few weeks later
slinging tavern beer
in a safe corner of the city

■ HEARTH OF DARKNESS
CALVIN WHARTON

Black coveralls, an old blue baseball cap,
and a persistent veneer of soot
compose this costume I wear

and drive through the city
in a Peugeot station wagon,
the back cluttered with brushes, ropes,
a vacuum-cleaner, and bags of ash
        already removed from concrete ashpits;

I imagine a link with William Blake,
visit the chimneys of North Vancouver
and clean each carefully
whether necessary or not;
perhaps more carefully
the ones that aren't really dirty,

and my boss
encourages me to encourage customers:
"more cleaning, this is a must,
don't forget the hazard of chimney fires"
but I refuse to advance his phony sales.

Although some people deserve
what they get,
like the woman who demanded to see my credentials,
and later apologized,
explained she only asked
because she thought I was a Negro.

■ SISTERS OF THE GARDEN
GERALD HILL

I vacuum under the pulpit
of the Catholic Church in Rocky Mountain House.
The only sound is a vacuum cleaner, a Kirby,
which I jostle against the carvings
of holy figures – they've been carved
and still for more than a hundred years.

The rugs are clean
and pure under the nuns' footsteps
on their way to water
plants upstairs. They're Sisters
of the Garden and silent
as leaves.

And I don't speak or violate
that stained glass light
or dust off any object
which might be a piece of the cross
(like my uncle did
at Notre Dame College in Wilcox, Sask.
The priest gave him *supreme* shit.)

I respect the confessionals
in Rocky Mountain House.
I store the Kirby in one of them
and whisper to it.

■ ICE
GERALD HILL

I drove away cool every morning
a 1981 white Dodge van a Ram 350
just another Dodge just
another f in traffic another blue bag

I parked like Hutterites with eggs
or dairy men with ice cream
letting the customers come to me
or I'd stand unloading blue bags
of ice five at a time into white
freezer boxes
                    somebody'd say
Got any ice? and I'd say *Yeah*
I got ice

        ■

I gazed at the RVs in Kelowna
from the west bank of Lake Okanagan
they were massed in the campsites
        clotheslines coolers and lawnchairs
        white legs and a dad

He'd just come the fifty miles from Penticton
        four bikes strapped to the grille
        two speedboats and a dinghy up top
        a couple of Hondas towed behind

113

food for thirty-five in the fridge
no wonder he was tuckered out
tinted cap or no tinted cap

■

Safeway was troubled by the ice business
out of their control
they had no supplier but me
                              I was Lord
of the Ice
              they only got their ice
when I chose to deliver

When I called the manager a can-stacker
                revolt of the can-stackers
                rebels in the aisles
I had to cool
              their uprising
had to twist it shut
                        at the source
I spoke to the manager
                        Cease!
Put down your phone I will deliver
the ice on time

■

Ice is gold
to the sunfolks
who go clammy in the mind
in the presence of ice

They stop their RVs to stare
              the strange blue glow of ice
they creep towards my truck
like fevered ones whose salve
has arrived
              I shout *Nurse!*
kindly administer these cubes
to the wounded

■

At the grocery store the white box
is empty when I arrive (the guy
standing there has already lost
a couple of dozen bags worth of sales)
I take my time backing up
I know what I'll hear
and I hear it
            Where the hell ya been?

Where the hell I been?
This is my third load today
buddy
and he says something at me
and it's cube against cube
it's icy stares and burn
        this icetruck Armageddon
Highway 97 south
                Penticton

        ■

I got iceman's elbow
        bruises on the elbow meaning rot
and old age telling me my cubes
on earth were numbered
                        I'll only stay
solid for a limited time

Once there was a nick
just a minor thing
but my finger split open
there was ice inside
chipped and bloody

I bumped my knee on a fender
I couldn't walk
it was a blue Merc'

■ WAITRESS
ALISSA LEVINE

I pick up the phone
and answer to a woman

that yes we are open
until ten at night

Thank you she doesn't say
"You're welcome."

     Water I bring them
     bread and wine
     They want salad
     I serve it
     and go back to the kitchen
     "Order in" I say
     and give in the bills

     Table four is up
     so's table five
     lasagna
     garlic bread
     Quiche Lorraine
     salmon
     perogies
     fries and gravy

     All served;
     I go 'round with the water
     (we call it watering the customers)

     Back to the kitchen
     my table is up

     two Specials
     done well
     a sour creamed baked potato
     on the side
     They want more wine

     I love to get my customers drunk.

     More wine all 'round
     Good.
     I hope they notice all the work

I'm doing for them

I expect tips.

At long last they go
or stay and have coffee
and talk and smoke cigarettes

I go 'round to refill
with coffee and cream
A woman passes her
cup to me

Thank you she doesn't say
"You're welcome."

■ THERE'S SOMETHING WRONG WITH MY SOUP
MARK McCAWLEY

Hey
I'm just
a busboy
        I told the manager
I don't know anything
about waitering
            but offering
        me a choice between
that or unemployment
and my rent due in two weeks
I donned the hated uniform
at the same time
a derelict woman sat and ordered
the soup of the day

No
sooner
had she eaten
        half the bowl
when she announced
to the lunch hour rush:
        "there's something wrong with my soup"
rushing over I apologize

quickly fetch her another
while throughout the room
other patrons look
to their soup

No
sooner
had she eaten
    half of that bowl
did she bellow again:
        "there's something very wrong with my soup
    I'm not paying for this"
other patrons refuse to eat
their soup and ask
for the manager
"What's
going on
here" shouts the manager
    "There's something wrong with the soup"
a chorus of customers reply
        "Mr. McCawley   what are you going
    to do about all this"
"Clear the tables?"

■ BUSBOY AND WAITRESS: CASHING OUT
JIM DANIELS

I sip my free drink with Karen,
my uniform stained with slop
from scraped plates, smelling
like a rancid buffet. I close my eyes,
and try to sigh deep enough. I hear
her splash the change onto the counter,
rustle her bills.

My face is tired, she says
pulling out her own stains –
a businessman's crude remark,
the visual undressing, some old ladies
who stayed forever, then stiffed her.
I wait for her to shove a little money my way,
nodding, listening – part
of what I'm paid for.

■ ADIEU
Marjorie Marks

Greasy food scraps embedded into the
    bottom of my shoes.
Newly-made dollar bills
    sticktogether.
The smell of boiled potatoes,
    burnt meat, fresh carrots.
Hands hot from scorched silverware,
    antiseptic rags.
Ears throb of MUZAK;
    cursing, hysteria – hysterical cursing.

Oh, to say goodbye
    to free food,
    broken rules,
    the lonely "regulars".
Five years of service to the hungry –
    gone.
The table is cleared.
Past tense is here.

■ DELI
Suzan Milburn

I
    number 46 please

they appear like phantoms
one minute no customers
the next
there are four   eight   fourteen
they stand staring
clutch their pink numbers
as we deliver
  package after package after package
of meat loaf   salami   ham

the plexiglass doors open and shut
                    open and shut
the slicer spits it out

       spits it out
         spits it out
in a space four feet by twenty
with three women whirling
as the scale
sticks out its tongue
with the printed price
     black forest ham $2.94
into a bag
and seal

     number 47 please
     can I help you
     with or without garlic
     will that be all

no conversation
amongst ourselves
not allowed

no conversation
with the customers
no time

and the meat
    the meat
    the meat

    the meat

  II
in slower moments I notice
the couples
as they stand before me
the showcase between

some
welcome me with their eyes
their clothes of comfort
show little shyness of colour
they touch
they laugh

I hear what he likes   she likes
            kid likes   dog likes

others
the woman is pressed against the case
and with the same insistence
her thighs push against polyester pants
she orders me
her eye on the scale
as her husband
leans on the cheese cooler
arms folded   ankles crossed
and discovers the ceiling

then there is the couple
where the man looks me in the eye
the woman   stands slightly behind
picks at the stitching in her coat
he jokes
talks about the weather
tells me what he wants
as I fill his order
I feel
her lowered eyes

    III
sometimes
when I'm pawing the meat ends
obliging
a taut lipped customer   who is pressed
against the deli case
their apologetic demands
set my jaw tight
indignation colours my cheeks
as I look for the not
too spicy
no rinds
only ham
no head cheese

        oh   and in three separate bags of 123 g

I imagine them
stark naked
hairy armpits
and a body marked
with the resentful red lines
of underwear

I smile
as I pass their package
over the case

    IV
the doors are locked
the shearing sound of dropped blinds
in the muted light
the atmosphere breathes again

      pull tickets
      clean spoons
      windex case
      cover meats
      clean slicer
      cash out

a relief
to be able to
just   work

aprons are peeled off
hair let down
finally
we can talk

begin to serve

ourselves

PUBLIC RELATIONS: DELAYED TRAIN, or THE ADDRESS OF THE PRESIDENT

Erin Mouré

This how nerve endings   stop
& turn;
continue as rails swollen-up by the sun,
treacherous:
The electric fibres, diesel generation of the brain,
generation of synapse, thought, the way
the passenger rep snapped at the passenger on Tuesday,
invoked his ancestors,
silent ones with their bones failing.

& the passenger cursed VIA,
howled at the railway, its blue diesel train pushing
the mainline between mountains,
14 hours behind schedule;
& he cursed
the crews whose hands ache with hours.

This is the way the nerve   endings   stop
& burn the slow atmosphere, slow
generation of oxygen, slow crumpled diesel thought
bent under stone
for centuries, the nerve   endings   stop
The train curls along the lake from Kamloops
The passenger rep snaps   *This is the address of the*
                         president. Write HIM a letter.

& turns, stopped
To the washroom to represent no one, her throat tight
with passengers,

with sick risings at 4 am
in major terminals, with dropped
switches, engine-brakes, pullman sleepers parked all night
in Vancouver station,
her throat stuck with arrivals
at 2 am on delayed train #3,
laughing-stock of the railway, its passengers fitful, the crews edgy,
41 hours payable in 2 days

■ NOT A TRAIN
Erin Mouré

When the girl hit the train window with the sledge,
breaking it into ice, she
frightened me, I held onto the sledge with both
hands whitening, glass in the roomette bed,
the train tilted, bent like
a moon rocket

The girl shifted & tied the bedsheet onto
the door,   when
she climbed out of the train window
onto the rocks of the river
she scared me
I picked up my duffle & kit & walked up
the twisted rails, my train tilted into the bank &
jackknifed, a moonscape,
the ties splintered, pieces of torn steel:
I was the girl who woke up
just before her train derailed, 2:45 am last August,
her body knowing what was wrong; it threw her
against the head-end of the roomette
& held her neck
surrounded by pure air &
the metal bending up into a branch of light
& fear
That's it, she thought
She knew the world was over, was over, was over,
who was she?

Hitting the train window from inside,
straining her arms against the force of the sledge,
kneeling on her bed, glass-filled,
six feet tall, courage, her second life
opening up.

The feel of it.
The feel of *not being trapped anywhere*.
The feel the ground made on her legs when
she dropped out of the train onto it, & looked back
to the metal she came from,
thinking   *A train moves, I am
not a train*

■ I DON'T PANIC STOP FOR (DING) BELLS
BRIAN PRATT

ding
i don't panic stop for bells
it's a rule i had to make up for myself
dingding
i panic stop for pedestrians cars all
manner of solid moving objects that position
themselves in front of my bus unexpectedly
even though i try to expect the unexpected
but i try not to panic stop for bells
dingdingding
that way i save lives discourage suicidal
dashes across traffic to
catch my bus
i watch them then pull away when they
are safely at my front door
dingdingdingding
so don't argue with me or take any number
down because i'm doing you a favour by not
stopping
it makes you a better passenger it slows
you down enough to know which bus you're
catching or to pay attention next time you
miss your stop
dingdingdingdingding
and everyone on board including me gets to where
we're going quicker fewer stops you see
dingdingdingdingdingding
but if i should lapse and make an effort
for someone when i didn't for another
all in the same trip and you're on the bus
to witness both actions
don't think of me as
ding-a-ling or dink
it really is a solid rule
i don't panic stop for bells
ding
oh geez
hang on everybody

■ SCHEDULES
BRIAN PRATT

they get on slow
   crippled
   old
   laden down
with their possessions
   their whole lives
packaged in borrowed bags

wheezing their diseases
passing the plague
   of their fractured lives
onto public transport
they smell of death
   decay
waxing the air thick

and i hate them

not for what they are
but because they
make me late

■ TO PROVE HIM WRONG
BRIAN PRATT

a comedian came on TV once
and pointed out that people
can speak of distance in time:
how far is it?
oh about a twenty minute drive
eight hours by jet
a two hour ferry ride
but you don't hear
time in terms of distance
except when I'm on the bus
people ask how late I am
and I look at my paddle
and then the street signs
and eventually after long computations

I'll say something like
six blocks

■ TEARDROPS ON THE ROAD
BRIAN PRATT

i keep my eyes on the road
so i won't hit anything
and i keep my eyes on the mirrors
so i know what's coming up
and i keep my eyes on the sidewalk
to watch out for people
and i keep my eyes on the speedometer
so i'm not going too fast
and i keep my eyes on the wires
because that's important to a trolley
and i keep my eyes on the pavement
because there are teardrops on the road
and if i could i'd keep a close watch
on this heart of mine
but i'll let johnny cash do that
because i have to keep my eyes on too many things
as it is

■ ROLLER COASTER
BRIAN PRATT

she got on again a few days later
sober
with a friend
talking about how lonely she had been
it was so bad she said
she even resorted to talking to the
bus driver

ah what's the use

people talk too loud
generally just think too loud

■ THEIR DISPATCH
DAVID BEAVER

they say it's better over there
the dispatch
administers the fleet
like a priest
with a flock of
poor sinners
under his wing
They say we work on the dark side
of the business
running wild
like a pack of
wolves
I don't mind living this way
I've got an illegal receiver
when I get tired of our excitement
I tune into their man
and take a few easy
trips

■ OUR DISPATCH
DAVID BEAVER

he's the star performer
in a circus act
riding the radio
waves like a
trained acrobat
juggling
names and addresses
He's a knife thrower too
knows the distance
I'll travel
to the target
I can't resist
I pick up the knife
he just threw at me
dull side up
It's a trip
          it's always a trip

          my hunger
     for a trip
I move off
into the night
losing his voice
but remembering all
the details

■ THE BROTHERHOOD
DAVID BEAVER

I like the people I work with
Charlie was gonna be
a rich man's son
but he couldn't fake it
Wolfie woulda made it in LA
playin rock and roll
but his dog bit off
a couple of his
pickin fingers
We don't complain much
about the workin conditions
we've got our eyes
on the prize
one day soon we're gonna hit
that safe Louie keeps
the company money in
we'll blow it through the window
hire a cab
and beat it to the airport
we'll go in style man
Yellow 69
or maybe even a
limo

■ THE POSTMAN
SADHU BINNING

in the dark
from the mouth of a radio clock
english words hit like a hammer
half opened eyes, unstable feet

from toilet to kitchen
dead silence
a cup of tea, a lunch bag
labelled clothes take control of your body

sorting mail for Jacksons, Sandhus and Yees
surrounded by people
who have learned life's secrets
from Donald Duck and Mickey Mouse
some of these 'brothers'
don't want to laugh with you
but at you
they don't even see you
they see an image
nailed in their minds
by the Creators of Donald and Mickey

letters in your hand
rain on your head
every dog is a lion in its house
crooked high stairs
the cats watch you and jump away
buried under fliers from Sears and Bays
your back screams
still you watch your steps
and they watch you
through their half open curtains
whites, blacks, indians, chinese
those kept in the house
have sharp eyes
some of them see you
as another somebody
who goes on strike just to trouble them

you deliver letters
that travel from your hand
to the garbage pail
what once was a tall and proud tree somewhere
piece by piece delivered to a garbage heap

you start with a handful

end with nothing
one year, two years and then you count no more
along the way your hairs change their colour
perhaps to make some white man happy
the rest remain the same to the end
yet piece by piece you deliver yourself

■ TOOLS OF MY TRADE
SUE SILVERMARIE

Midstride today my spine twitches
The message?
Switch the pouch!
I lift it over to my other shoulder
so its 35 pounds
tug muscles and backbone
in the opposite direction. Ah.
Awkwardly I learn
lefthanded fingering and delivery.

After work my feet
seem like stumps.
I climb slowly
to my second floor flat.
At each step heels throb.
They weren't built
to pound concrete!
While supper cooks
I learn the holy points
where acupressure heals my soles.

Throughout this ten hour day
I've traded my body for a wage.
With spine and shoulders,
hands and knees and feet,
I've created a living for my family.
Dear tools of my trade,
can you forgive the abuse?
I toughen you by day.
Each evening, I honour your needs.

■ FEDERAL OFFENCE
SUE SILVERMARIE

During a week of Training we saw
film after film of employees caught.
If it wasn't an Inspector in the crawlspace
built above every workroom floor,
it was one watching from a phone booth
or in an unmarked car along the route.
One slip and the Inspector would pounce.

Most of these soaps
climaxed with the clang of a jail cell,
pitiful employee sagging against the bars,
staring into the camera with remorse.

After a week of such fables
I couldn't sleep, I saw Federal Offences
hidden everywhere like land mines.
Riddled with subliminals no doubt, those films.
Right from the start they had me,
afraid of losing my coveted spot
at the bottom of hierarchy's heap.

It took a year for the Training dose to wear
and my common sense to return.
The first time I committed a Federal Offence
I didn't have much choice.
Bloods came down heavy as I carried Route 23,
so I sneaked home to change hoping my jeep
with its code number painted front and back
wouldn't be reported OUTSIDE THE ZONE!

After that there was no turning back.
Defiance fired me as I READ A POSTCARD!
Wishing I were there too,
I propped it up in the corner of my lettercase
to bring mountains into my fluorescent morning.

Then after a carrier in Kansas was raped
and it was time for the night collection,

I actually allowed my girlfriend
to RIDE ALONG in the Postal truck!

Finally I shook off
the Training paranoia for good.
Boldly I WORE A BUTTON to work!
My boss and I fought for an hour
over whether "Nuclear-Free Future"
came under the Manual's definition
of political endorsement.
"Take it off or I'll write you up,"
he yelled, by this time red
over my commie insubordination.

Calmly, I told him to go ahead.
No more wondering when,
I smiled to think it had happened.
At last I was caught
committing a Federal Offence.
And one I could be proud of.

■ **AFTER ALL**
SUE SILVERMARIE

At the bottom of the porch steps
I freeze in an icy sprawl
clutching my shin.
My cry hangs like an icicle in the air
but no one emerges.
No one drives by.
No one so much as peeks from behind curtains.
Snow falls on scattered letters.

I breathe. Step one,
remove mailbag from shoulder.
Step two, roll up pants to inspect damage.
No blood, no break
bad scrape, ugly bruise tomorrow.

Time to rise. After all,
this is just the first block.

■ STANDARDS

SUE SILVERMARIE

When FASTER was our boss's constant prod,
Joe showed me a standard
of real success on the job.
He put being friendly above being fast.
When Joe was through with his own route
he'd look me or another sub up
to deliver a block or two of ours.
He got us through Probation that way,
said he was passing along
what someone had done for him.

On the #14 bus that we both rode home
we'd talk a little every day.
He told how he missed the country life,
how he dreamed of raising horses.
When I asked him how he could keep so even
despite a family trouble or two,
he answered, "Just as well laugh as cry."
And, "Ain't got no use for fussin'."

When the boss started in one day
on moving more feet of mail per hour,
how we weren't reaching "Time & Work Standards
as defined in Methods Handbook M-41,"
Joe said low from the back,
"The wind's blowin' now, but lies
from a no-count don't addle me none."
The boss never did figure out
why all the carriers were grinning.

Joe wasn't rocked by the boss's demands
and he refused to be a mail machine.
He was proud to serve his customers
and to treat his co-workers, every one,
by his own high HUMAN standards.
Management called him a Commie.
To me he was a man of calibre
bureaucracy couldn't bring down.

from EVER TOOK ME SERIOUSLY AS A CPR COP
<small>KEN RIVARD</small>

1
during my training
sergeant major asks what I would do
if someone starts shooting at me.
I reply: DUCK.
he says: NO, you should get down on one knee like this
and he lowers himself behind his desk,
his right index finger like a pistol.
then he says: POW, POW, POW,
leave as little target as possible.
POW, POW, POW? I ask.
yes, don't forget POW, POW, POW, he says.
I tell myself to remember
to always have a desk
following me around
on my beat.

4
in my uniform for the first time
I try to ride city transit for free
just like the city cops do
but I get caught when the bus driver
reminds me I'm not a city cop
and the wool of my baggy pants
makes me think
I'll end up paying
for this job.

7
out at Seagram's I'm like a watchman again
checking boxcar seals
to make sure booze is safe.
suddenly I hear a noise
and
another.
the sweat beneath my wool pants is too much.
night then lets loose a ragged set,
a ragged set of vocal chords:
it's only Sergeant Sirois, son,

just checking to make sure
you're on your toes.
CPR policemen should always
be on their toes
RIGHT, son?

8

on my beat at CP Express a driver motions to me
to get outside, fast.
there, I see a man pulling a woman by her arm
across the CPR parking lot.
I figure I should do something.
first, I yell: STOP.
then I blow my whistle.
next I flash my flashlight,
you know,
like they do on television.
I finally have to run up to them and say: HOLD IT.
that works.
he tells me he's taking his drunken wife home.
she says it's not true
and pulls up her skirt
showing bruise-covered thighs.
he beat me up outside a bar, she says.
what am I supposed to do? asks a voice.
believe it or not I'm able to flag down
a city police cruiser.
it works.
since I'm no longer on CPR property,
it's over.
I walk back across to the CPR parking lot
and I don't know how to laugh
at being afraid
of my own fears.

■ FLYING THE NIGHT FREIGHT
ROBERT GARRISON

Smooth air up here tonight,
For sure.
I have those instrument lights turned down
To dimly glowing fireflies;

The solemn instrument dial faces relate
Empirical messages in the dim red light.

Navigating a familiar route
Under an almost-full moon and
A clear winter sky,
I like to hear the steady engine, of course,
But I also like to listen to the rush of cold air
Slipping past this aluminum sky canoe.

I don't particularly mind that my hands and feet
Are chilly,
Or even that I'm tired of sitting
So long.
Tonight I have this old Cessna airplane
Tuned up – like a violin or a fine piano.
At eleven thousand feet I'm giving
A regular cold-air recital.

■ WORKING ALONE
ANDREW VAISIUS

The lab sings when I am alone in it
sometimes to the metronome tick of the timer
if I have a timed test running
otherwise, the different pitched hums from the pump
of the liquid chromatographic system provide backing
and the air bubbling through the constant temp. water bath
of the dissolution apparatus is jerky enough
to be jazzy.
The dishwasher changes cycles with a thud and chugs
through a drain and rinse.

I hear these things alone among molecules
smile inwardly at the intellect which separates
those million atomic formations into their likes
and not-alikes.

Is it magic to take a tablet, crush it
soften it and dissolve some of its constituents
in an organic solvent,
filter that solvent and shoot a slug of it

into another phase of solvents flowing
through a C_{18} column housed in steel.

The slug separates.
Larger molecules go charging through
while the smaller ones bounce around and come out later.
They flow past an ultraviolet light
of a particular wavelength
and absorb some of its energy while passing.
This is seen as electrical noise
and depicted as peaks on a linear graph.

Is it really all science and math and no magic?
The peaks quantified and measured against a standard
of a chemically pure substance.

The magic is in the wonder that thousands of people
in separate workplaces
fiddling with theories and method development,
designing and constructing fantastic apparatus
and elegant glassware,
people formulating and pressing and packaging
these pharmaceutical tablets,
have come together in their results
finally in my workplace.

Right now, it's a veritable symphony
but I alone
hear its molecular notes.

■ **JOYCE JOSEPHSON**
KIRSTEN EMMOTT

"This young primigravida, a patient of Dr. Adey's,
for whom I was on call,
telephoned me on the morning of September 4th
in labour,
came to the hospital about 2100 hours,
was found to be about 7 centimetres dilated with the head at
    the spines.
After a rapid transition stage
and an uneventful second stage

she was delivered of a healthy boy
at about one a.m. on September 5th.
Postpartum course was uneventful."

It was a routine case.
Only a short time to sip coffee in the quiet lounge
hearing the midnight murmurings of hospital halls
waiting for the little one to come down
Only a short time to sit, hands on lap, on the metal stool
waiting for the little one to come down
to flop, squirming, onto my green gowned lap and be lifted
(the bright lights turned politely away)
gurgling onto his mother's belly
her hands turning the wet skin pink as little lungs filled –

The new father bowed his head by hers and wept
unconsoled by her queenly smile.

These three, bound together in holy love,
forgot all about me
as I quietly stitched, cleaned up, ungowned and tiptoed out.

Before these routine miracles
we must all bow down
and dictate case summaries to tell
how uneventfully
the wondrous gift is given.

■ NO FEAR OF BLOOD
Kirsten Emmott

I have to be careful about suede or canvas shoes,
for once you get blood on them it's hard to get it out.
Even in scrub boots you can't always protect your feet
from the cascade of blood that follows the birth of the placenta
or worse, at Caesarean section, the opening of the uterus
and the blood and amniotic fluid pour down her side
and onto your shoes
especially if you are standing on the assistant's side
to which the belly is always tilted:
Anyway, you can't very well say to the shoe salesman,
Something suitable for wading in blood, please.

Taking the newborn child on your lap
results in a wet and sometimes bloody lap.
Manual removal of a placenta
means a bright red glove of blood.
Cutting the cord, which is under pressure between the clamps,
results in a spray of blood, right in your eye if you're not
    careful.

You have to clean up pretty carefully before leaving the
    delivery room,
lest the next tour of pregnant couples
peering about the delivery suite
get a shock at the sight of you.

    II
The blood of birth, which is normal, which nature builds up
    slowly
in generous amounts over nine months, ready to be harmlessly
    shed,
is beautiful.

It's the most beautiful red there is.
And the hot red blood smells good, it's a strange animal smell,
odd the first time you notice it.

Most people think it's crazy
to have no fear of blood and its smell
of women and their lively flavours
but not me.

I love the smell of labouring women, the amniotic fluid that
soaks the bed, their earthy beauty.

■ JUNKIE / MOTHER
KIRSTEN EMMOTT

The social worker's note began,
"This hostile, bitter young woman..."

My note began,
"Premature labour
at thirty weeks' gestation."

No, she didn't want to take the drugs
to stop the labour.
No, she didn't want to be examined.
No, she didn't care about the baby.
She drove us away with curses.

And when she cursed the infant into my hands
when she saw what she had done
then came tears.
"Oh, God, he's so little.
He's so little.
You better live, you little fucker,
You better live!"

She went out on Methadone
but within four weeks
stopped coming to see him
didn't answer the phone any more
and when she did, she sounded sleepy...

He lies in his incubator
where we stroke him and whisper to him
of adoption and love.

Who knows how much fear
he has already known
curled up in bitter darkness
already saying in sad dreams
oh, mother, don't do it,
don't do it.

■ JOB DESCRIPTION
ALICIA PRIEST

care for Mr. Crystal:
salute his eye
caress him
lift his head
to take the juice
slide the soap
along his thigh
stroke his shoulder-bone

and follow down
to powder folded loins
sting his tongue
with sweetened lemon
sweep his lips
with vaseline
dress him turn him
roll him in your arms

then
with your finger-tips
draw out his teeth
press shut his eyes
wind his ring off
and send it to the safe
tie a tag
around his toe
and another round
the plastic bag
shove him on a stretcher
and wheel him to the fridge
orderly help push
it's cold down here
hurry: hurry
close the door
kill
the lights

■ WORKING WHILE OTHERS SLEEP
ALICIA PRIEST

I love with a secret joy to watch
over the sick as they sleep – the
halls tunnelling into darkness, the doctors
banished at last to their beds, the
night opening like a desert before me.

I enter the room, flashlight
dead in my hand, and there the moon dances
on four silent faces.

How beautiful you all are.
Even you Mr. Willoughby, face divided
in day by bitterness, a mind unforgiving
of its body, even you
can't help yourself fall
like an infant angel into the
lap of the mother.
Your face on the pillow, a
flower, can no longer hide the
tenderness you've denied ever having.

And you McPhee, your creased hand crooked
in the corner of your neck,
fingers curled like a fiddlehead around
some forest shadow. I want
to slip my hand in yours and
feel the river of dreams returning.

But Henry, you are my favourite,
in sleep you fall so far that
everytime I hear you take in the night
and then give it back
I leave the room brimming
with the mystery of sleeping life.

■ THE UNCONSCIOUS PATIENT
ALICIA PRIEST

neurologically
semi-comatose
we don't know
what he hears or if
he hears at all
dropped dead
beside the Ladies Auxiliary
heart stopped
we zapped him
and it started
but who knows how long
his brain breathed
without oxygen

he'll live
so long as he's hooked up
but he could be hearing every word
we say
I've known them to wake up
and repeat whole conversations
so be careful
the room is bugged

■ SEEING LAZARUS
ALICIA PRIEST

Just once
I would like to see Lazarus
appreciated

One standing ovation
for the dead
come to life
for the reversal of the normal
order of things
a movie played backwards:
he lives he dies he
lives he walks
the line

Or even honourable mention
in the obituary column
after the buried
(in fine print)
come the resurrected

Instead, we who
raise the dead
go on
inspecting ears
sewing fingers
eating lunch
no one sees Lazarus

Me, I'm in trouble
during resuscitation

I sense a third presence
see a shadow cross
the turning face of him
whose death is turned
twitching into life

■ READING THE ENTRAILS
GLEN DOWNIE

They warned me it can be dizzying to look down
into an open man   They joked
that I should be sure to fall
backwards off the stool if I felt faint
But you get used to it

after the shock of that first deliberate
slice into soft pink
fine and clean as a paper cut
when the blood comes quick and alive to the sleeping flesh
and trails the delicate silver blade
down to the tough white backing
which must be scored and stabbed
before it splits like a tight sack

exposing the jelly layer   the fat yields easily
and deep   the slashed capillaries leaking blood
into the crevice   So they take what looks like
a dainty soldering iron and sizzle the bright ends
black and neatly shut so the knife can descend
to the stretched red corset of muscle
which is ripped and held open with brute force
that should wake the dead

and you know then
this is no joke   There seems no limit
to the violence they will use
against the wholeness of a man
to save his life   They're sure
they're right to do it

Their gloved hands were in the pit of him past the wrist
and he lost his face for a while

as I was absorbed in his guts
all lumpy wet pink tubes and yellow sacks
with the rubber fingers slipping and digging around
like someone rummaging in a cluttered purse
for a key   I forgot his face
till the knife nicked one wet sack

and a spurt like tobacco juice splattered on my shoe
I saw him again then   eyes shut
his breathing regular
and the stubble of shaved belly hairs
darkening as the antiseptic dried

It was morning outside the room   A winter sun
yawned in the window
A hose slurped up the spill
in the gash of his body
where I could see no answer
to the stranger's open question
only pieces of him being slopped into metal bowls

■ GRIEVING
GLEN DOWNIE

The door opens to light weak as watered sun
She lowers herself as though wounded
into a chair

She has written strange letters accusing
the doctors   the hospital   *The man in the coffin*
was grim-faced   My husband
was gentle
You listen helpless while she chases
her conspiracy tale
The ragged scrap story
whirls around like a dust devil

and slams shut all possible doors
till the room has collapsed
suddenly silent and close as a breathless lung
In her fear she is wearing
the grim face her husband –
No   Never

Her husband was gentle
and vanished impossibly
cleansed of all shadow
like a letter unwriting itself
like a bed sheet unwrinkling

and you are a weak door
she opens and closes again
There is only this wounded light
left to grieve for the body

■ LOUISE
GLEN DOWNIE

The nurses say I'm glad my mother died
quickly   I'd never go
into one of those homes   Promise me
you'll shoot me if I get like that

Louise is *like that*   Sitting on the commode
she bleats the length of the hall
Take me to the bathroom   Take me. . .
Take me. . .

They tell her You're on the toilet   It's OK
She whimpers Is this the chair where I can let go?
Her panic   her desperate dignity
contort her features
Is this it? Can I let go?
Can I let go?

Yes Louise   This is it
It's all right to let go
Let go now
before hospital policy changes
and nurses patrol the wards with guns in their hands
tracking down their own echoes:
Shoot me if I get like that

■ PROSTHETICS
GLEN DOWNIE

He gives me eyes
to stare back at

hands me a nipple
he made himself

He admits that sometimes
his people are disappointed

He has to remind them
gently
he isn't God

though he's laboured longer
on the blues of an iris
or an ear's
curled
mystery

The spare parts man
does brave work

but he shies away
from my praise

When he gives me his hand
it's warm
and his smile is genuine

■ MR. PETRIE
PHIL HALL

I was paged by Sister Michaux,
the young, shy podiatrist,
fat-faced, in rimless glasses –
the nun who was always making eyes
at my soul.

She wanted me

to help her open Mr. Petrie's door.
He had not come to Mass.

I knew we would find him drinking rye
and tap water. He was
dead, his false teeth: objects,
his drink: sharp pieces.

I picked him up off the wet floor,
my partner in crimes that were not crimes,
old winker.

Would you believe
anything?

As I held the dead man
Sister Michaux was making eyes
at my soul.

I wanted to wink at her right then,
for both of us, kicking and goner,
but I am not that strong.
I had to put Mr. Petrie down.

That's how I missed my chance
to be eternally damned.

■ **ANSWERS**
KIRSTEN EMMOTT

How did you feel when you had your baby?
Right there.

Were you frightened?
No.

Did it hurt?
It was like being hugged too hard.

What did your husband do?
He was there.

What did your father do?
He held my son.

What did your mother do?
She held the mirror.

How much did the baby weigh?
She was weightless.

What time was she born?
She was timeless.

How did you feel when you held her?
Ready.

■ **NEWBORN**
ZOË LANDALE

It is not light I rise to now
        but her face
   tiny   a coin
winking in sun
     blink and I groan again,
        plead for more sleep,
   time, five minutes even

The child swims   up from her carriage;
        acrylic blankets riffle   soft   pastel
   to the bed.
            My hands pluck roars from
   air thick with exhaustion.

            I loathe clocks, they never give me
room between hours anymore.

Through the cycle of her
   vehement needs,
        I lag behind my hands.
   Caretakers, they pull me to
        act out love, gentle
in the grainy space remaining from nurture,
   rooms darkened for sleep at noon;
fresh cream smell of her.

I could not sleep after she was born.
    Out the hospital window,
  the night-time city rumbled,
       sky pink with reflected lights
and her face swung before me
    one grave eye open,
        the other gummed with amniotic fluid;
baby   a lit medallion
me   astonished
      repeating   her face

■ *RAVAGED*: A LOVE POEM
MARY DI MICHELE

Waking with her body
folded into the hollow of mine,
back to belly like twin fetuses,
myself the elder by moments,
or like a model of a pregnant mother,
the belly mound peeled back and the baby
out in the world but still connected,
the umbilical cord that was not buried
in the ground with the afterbirth
an artery to my heart,
my hand on my daughter's midriff,
stroking skin silkier than even
the lids of eyes,
finds the first bump.
        In the light I see the red blister
of chicken pox.
      It spreads.
It *ravages* her face
        although I feel wrong
to use that word which makes romance
of rape, sonorous with *a*'s,
resonating to make a private, lurid act,
a history. She seems suddenly thrust
into adolescence, her skin a victim
of sex glands.
       Ten long days of quarantine,
one grueling night of fever through which she cries
the open-mouthed cries of Italian syllables I heard

when she was pulled from my body
royal with the blood of birthing,
by the technician's hands, the doctor
who had threatened to cut her out
like the appendix lost years before.

For days my breasts failed to respond
to those cries, the word *love*
like an Adam's apple in a woman's throat,
and bottles of honeyed water,
and nipples bleeding from those hard sucking gums
and no milk.

On this night I feel mother enough,
but she needs more than anyone
can give her as the blisters break.
She can't sit down or lie still.
The burning makes her writhe
like an eel swimming against the current,
and I carry her now and rock her,
head spent against my shoulder
and my crooning and care
are the few sandbags I build
against the flood.
Her pain and my helplessness.
Love is a placebo.
                    Up to a point,
it seems to work.

■ "WHO LOOKS AFTER YOUR KIDS?"
Kirsten Emmott

"Who looks after your kids when you work?"
"Who does the housework?"
"How do you manage working those long hours with a family?"
"How do you manage with the kids?"

Well, there's their father, and a nanny and a day care centre
but they don't really hear, the people who ask.
They don't want to know about it.

What they want to hear is:

Who does the housework? My henpecked worm of a husband. Me,
until four in the morning. A Jamaican wetback whom we
    blackmail
into slaving for peanuts. Nobody, we all live in a huge
    tattered
ball of blankets like a squirrel's nest.

Who bakes the bread? Never touch it. Mac's Bakery. The
    pixies.
A little old Irishwoman named Kirsten Emmott comes in every
    week.

How do you manage with the kids? I don't. I neglect them.
I'm on the verge of a nervous breakdown, please help me.
I'm drinking heavily. I don't give a damn about the kids,
let them go to hell their own way.

Who looks after the kids? Nobody, I tie them to a tree in
the back yard every day. My senile old grandmother. The
Wicked Witch of the West.

■ FEAR OF FAILURE
DALE ZIEROTH

Her first time on skis,
and the first real snow this winter,
she is unhappy with the spotlight, the snow, the very
air in her lungs: can't bend her knees
perfectly
right away – this is Five Years Old and I try to help
but the snow seems to be too much for us:
she whacks me on the knee
ski pole on cold bone
and I grab her and she cries
and I'm mad now cause I've done that wrong
and my record for being the kind of father I want to be
is still too few days.
And later I try to
explain but I must hold too tightly cause she
spins away and it's finished for her anyway, she
decides to take up skating while I
go over the words again: Look

Nobody's Good Right Away
At Anything
printing or putting on clothes or even
breathing: it's gotta be shaken out of you.
And I can't believe a man can stumble so much
with his child and just because she's alive
sure I believe in miracles
but what about when my blood goes numb
when the world rumbles and pains in the press
or the everyday lives make no headlines and die
choked on the pain all the way
or the endless complaints of money and sweat and
kids spitting at each other on the way to school
the taste of gas like death in the air.
I sit and listen to the future.
Do you know how it feels yet?
Do you sometimes feel it, little kid, little kid,
red coat against the snow, a
toboggan full of smiles, shake me
shake me loose, join me to the day:
I lack the drive
I slide down past the handholds of home
and I manage and scarcely care today
where the melting snow goes or takes me or ends.

■ THE DEATH OF THE VIOLIN
DALE ZIEROTH

. . . in our house came after four years.
She had practised – and not practised –
long enough to (finally) make music.
She had entertained my father and mother,
and I had been proud of the songs
she had coaxed from those harsh strings.
She was, however, not staying with it.
We could no longer continue with
reminders, because reminders would be
nagging, and we wanted discipline
on her part: we wanted her to bring her will
into play.

November is a hard month to give up anything,
especially if you have held it
four years, watched it grow in your arms
until you knew just how
to make the music leap.
My own father's violin hangs on the wall
and I remember when he played,
touching the strings, jabbing
at the notes until the instrument
became a fiddle, and around him
guitars and accordions
filled up the family with their talk.

Once, when she played,
his violin played back,
reverberating on the wall: just once
there was that calling note. Then silence.
Filled up now with rain,
the arguments (about who's supporting whom
through this decision) that last their time
and fade, but stay, fill the air
and are cast back slowly into the pit
of all old family fights,
where the world gets drained off to
when it lurches and
can't move gently into change
and someone's disclaiming all reason
and another's volume rises to the shriek.

■ **GRADE NINE**
EVELYN GRAYSON

Thirty-eight against one.
I play ogre.

Paul sit down
Mary turn around
Henry get to work
Jamie what page are we on?
Why don't you know?
Bev I said STOP TALKING

nag, nag, old stoneface
and their eyes gratefully follow
a whizzing bee, official distraction
of the moment

George, give me that book
you do English in English class
Laura tosses a red pen to Maureen
giggles and clock-watching
The ogre grows teeth, turns green

Later, there are smiles
greetings in the sociable hallways
flustered excuses for books left at home
pleases and thank yous

I am amazed.

The ogre slams them against the wall
yet they bounce like India rubber
almost
enjoying the game

ON BEING TEACHER REP IN THE STUDENT SWIMATHON

ROBERT CURRIE

for Gisele and Anne

After ten laps
I wallow on my back
The echo on the rafters
is my gasping breath
and you are passing me
the two of you
teen-aged trim   sleek
as pickerel

I plough along your wake
You both have passed again
Forgetting where I am
I strike the pool's end

Through my thinning hair
I rub the lump that forms
shake the water from my specs
While hanging on the rope
that marks our lane
I think about a heaving brontosaurus
helpless in another time

The two of you
are churning up the water
exuberant as dolphins
kicking off the end again
Smiles and waves
that I should carry on

Forty laps to go
and I will follow
your white and flashing heels

from THE CHALKBOARD POEMS: THE MAGNATES

GLEN SORESTAD

The staffroom phone is their lottery
and each time it is dialled, or beckons them
their stock market nerves jangle together.

They move through their days like merchants
wired to the telex of their Wall Street dreams
and make imaginary bonanzas of every ring.

In the classroom, away from brokers' phones
they assign busy-work, sit in their desks
and calculate wishful profits on foolscap.

They build cabins at northern lakes, hit Las Vegas,
buy apartment blocks, sell houses, buy gold – *on paper*
and turn profits that will free them forever.

When the day's last buzzer sounds its reprieve
they flee before the crush of students to the halls
drawn like corporate magnates to the waiting calls.

■ from **THE CHALKBOARD POEMS: THE CARP**

GLEN SORESTAD

Over morning coffee he bubbles with issues,
has answers for all the thorny questions,
cures for each assorted ill of education.

But when the issues come before the staff
he crouches behind a wall of silence –
nothing distinguishes him from the dead.

When forced to speak before us all
he dons a painful blank of non-commitment
and crippled words lurch away from him.

But next day at coffee, like Lazarus he is back
and glows with eloquence, issue after issue –
a veritable repository of pedagogical bullshit.

from **THE CHALKBOARD POEMS: MOONLIGHTER**

GLEN SORESTAD

Moonlighter teaches by day
and works in a bar until 2:00

Mortgaged to the hilt with a mansion
his wife simply had to have
they have filled it with seven kids
and another is due in the spring

Today he could not even buy
the house he now lives in
and his mortgage rate has doubled
so he lives on five hours sleep

Each day his face grows greyer
as he moves toward the final bell

from THE CHALKBOARD POEMS: EFFICIENCY EXPERT

GLEN SORESTAD

His time is metronomic – every second
accounted for in his daily log.
Spontaneity is not tolerated.
His classes run like quartz movements:
activities flash like commercials
across his video days. Students are synchronized.
He would love to program their thoughts
and often believes that he has
but his students have their own buttons
and turn him off at will.

COLLEGE

RON MILES

Twelve years of working
together, liking each other
less or not at all
have taught us
more than years of school

that students fail instructors
procrastinate deadlines
wait

that much-talked revolution
isn't imminent (or wished)
that the current student crop's
the weakest ever

that teaching never changes
has changed, is not
what one expected

that old lectures move smoothly

that there isn't enough money isn't
enough money isn't enough

that teachers learn a part
of what they preach,
                              always
another hopeful
face at the door.

■ STUDENTS
Tom Wayman

The freshman class-list printouts
showed birthdates so recent
Wayman was sure the computer was in error.
One young man, however, was curious
about Wayman's mention near the start of term
of his old college newspaper:
"You were an editor *when?* Wow,
that's the year I was born."

The wisdom of the students
hadn't altered, though.
Wayman observed many clung to
The Vaccination Theory of Education
he remembered: once you have had a subject
you are immune
and never have to consider it again.
Other students continued to endorse
The Dipstick Theory of Education:
as with a car engine, where as long as the oil level
is above the add line
there is no need to put in more oil,
so if you receive a pass or higher
why put any more into learning?

At the front of the room, Wayman sweated
to reveal his alternative.
"Adopt The Kung Fu Theory of Education,"
he begged.
"Learning as self-defence. The more you understand
about what's occurring around you
the better prepared you are to deal with difficulties."

The students remained skeptical.
A young woman was a pioneer
of The Easy Listening Theory of Learning:
spending her hours in class
with her tape recorder earphones on,
silently enjoying a pleasanter world.
"Don't worry, I can hear you,"
she reassured Wayman
when after some days he was moved to inquire.

Finally, at term's end
Wayman inscribed after each now-familiar name on the list
the traditional single letter.
And whatever pedagogical approach
he or the students espoused,
Wayman knew this notation would be pored over
with more intensity
than anything else Wayman taught.

■ MARKING
Tom Wayman

I begin each essay with a calm mind –
a fresh start.
But as I consider what they have written
I get angry: the most cursory of rereadings
would have caught this sentence fragment,
and here is a misused semicolon
after we spent more than an hour on that in class
and where I talked to this student individually
for another thirty minutes about this persistent mistake.
And instead of the simple structure of the expository paper
which we have also gone over and over
and which can be so helpful a model, a technique, a guide,
here again is a jumbled series of random observations:
trite, contradictory, obviously hurried
and spelled wrong.

My red pencil becomes enraged.
It stalks through the words,
precise, bitter, vindictive,
acting as if it is pleased to discover error

and pounce on it, hacking and destroying and rearranging,
furiously rooting out sloppiness and weakness
as though upholding some stern moral precept
against another, softer age.

But the hand gripping the pencil
begins to tremble with remorse.
It feels it has led the students on
to try to express themselves
and then betrayed them:
attacking what they have exposed
of their ideas and emotions.
What use is righteousness, the hand wishes to ask the pencil,
without charity?

I read the name at the top
and think of the young person whose effort this is.
Now all I see on the paper
is a face, crestfallen when I hand back what they attempted.
Eyes look up at me
apprehensively, as at a judge.
We both know my weighing of their skill
will be taken to be an assessment of themselves.

It is as though I have been asked to mark
not essays but their faces,
not sentences but who they are.
I raise my pencil, but my hand still shakes.
I want to show them what in normal English usage
is considered incorrect.
But I can not assign a grade to their eyes.

■ SHOW
JIM DANIELS

In a class full of smooth faces
hers cracked into lines like my mother's.
She turned in a rhyming poem
called "Drunk Drivers Go To Jail."
It preached about how God would
get them for killing innocent people.

I told her "Don't preach."
She said "My son was killed
by a drunk driver. That's
truth. It's what I feel."
I gave her the standard advice:
"Show don't tell. Image over abstraction."

She brought in pictures of her son
and a pile of his clothes,
dumped them on my desk
with a drop slip.
I rubbed my hands
over a worn pair of jeans.

■ FOR KIRSTEN EMMOTT, DOCTOR & POET
PHIL HALL

In Delivery skill takes over:
the doctor saves the baby boy – unusual baby

but a beautiful poem the doctor writes about him

and reads tonight, and begins to cry –
another skill taking over

THE AGING FLIGHT INSTRUCTOR BRACES – NOT UNNOTICEABLY – FOR A BAD LANDING BY AN ENERGETIC STUDENT
ROBERT GARRISON

He mutters, as resourceful as possible,
"Add power, add power –
Goddamnit, give it full throttle!"

He thinks: ". . . Hate to lose it like that –
Now look at the kid's white knuckles."

Uneasiness is a hot ball of wax to be passed
Back and forth between student and instructor.

"Now," his voice once more calm as the light plane
Gains secure altitude,

"You see, when you've bounced once and the plane
Is headed back in nose-low, you must add power.
Now let's try again. This time keep the airspeed
On 60 on final – you were 75 or so last time."

Later, the aging instructor who had braced
Not unnoticeably, for the bad landing
By an energetic student recalled when Ben Sorenson,
His instructor, took not *one* but *two*
Bounces before flipping out

And inside all of those students there lurks
A frozen rabbit
Which turns the instructors white like wintertime.

■ DOOR TO DOOR FOR A TENANT'S UNION
DAVID MCKAIN

Six days in a row below zero.
We pamphlet through a sea-captain's house,
broken to apartments.
In the hall through waterstains,
lead-base paint and scaling plaster
we could see a sinking ship.
The mocha walls and brown linoleum,
they're colours from the bottom.

We climb stairs to a cell
under the widow's walk
where a woman eighty lives alone.
She can't climb stairs and has no phone
so when we knock, she clasps her hands
and sings it's Christmas.

Inside, listening to how cold it gets
at night, we sip coffee with our coats on:
a pan of water freezes by her bed.

She says she came from Ireland
without anybody – no mother, no father,
but like a pretty penny, found a job,
a live-in housekeeper for a doctor.

They kept her twenty years.
She says this, her eyes wide and shining.

Smiling, she says it doesn't matter.
She doesn't want the trouble we call help.

THE WORK OF LOOKING FOR WORK
WORK
Unemployment

■ WARNINGSIGNS
SUSAN EISENBERG

Harsh tongues
          soften; gentler tempers
ignite on contact. Rumours
reproduce on the hour –
   Bobby swears seven / Dave heard four /
   Steve is definite: three today
                    five next Friday.

                  At coffee
John swallows his hot and
   jumps back to work;
Kenny whines about why a
   just-married guy needs a job most;
Curt lectures on "what he
   never liked about this wormshop."

Much as a farmer smells an approaching storm
an experienced mechanic can
taste it in the morning coffee break:

layoff today.

■ from JOB WRUNG POEMS: 4
PENNY PIXLER

Friday layoffs:
Monday after the massacre,
the parking lot was so empty
I looked at my watch:
was I that early?

■ E-WAY COUNTER
LEON E. CHAMBERLAIN

In the old days –
   every time I passed the sign,
   the numbers were revolving.
Counting off new cars being built.
   These busy little numbers never rested.

They whirled into the millions every year,
methodically rolling over and over,
in quest of record sales.

Click! a new Mercury off the line at Wayne.
Click! a new Cadillac from Fleetwood Body.
Click! another Charger out of Jefferson Avenue.
Click! a Vega from Lordstown.

Whenever I drove by,
    day or night,
    it was clicking off cars.
Driving by on a Sunday afternoon
on a beautiful summer day,
after visiting Grandma
        they rotated. Click!
        The same on New Year's Day. Click!
        On Christmas Eve. Click!
        On Turkey day. Click!
        The assembly lines were always moving.
        Click! Click! Click!
The numbers always turned.
        Slowly and steadily.
Somebody out there was buying a lot of new cars.

What a proud industry.
We were a sleeves-rolled-up, gritty bunch.
A no-nonsense, get 'em out, people-want-cars type
of crew.
The arsenal of Democracy.
The supervisor said:
"Do you want to make forty grand this year?
Well, work seven days a week, twelve hours a day.
We need you, man, to build these cars."
It felt good to be needed.

We didn't want Texas' jobs.
People came from all over the USA for our jobs.
    And we welcomed them.
We were generous. There was work for all.
People wanted every car we could build.
The factories laboured seven days a week.

Twenty-four hours a day
the machines howled and belched smoke.
They never stopped.
    Yet people wanted more cars.

And therein lies the message.
People bought anything
            and everything.
Good or bad, somebody bought it.
Even the junk and scrap.

So management said:
    "Speed 'em up –
    we can sell more –
    it's an unlimited market –
    if we burn Joe –
    Sam is waiting in line behind him."
    But Soichiro was waiting behind us all

Suddenly, it went flat
    like a blowout.
    A complete reversal –
    a 180-degree turn –
    the belly-flop of a tough industry
    a proud industry.
    The arsenal of democracy.
    From weekend warriors and seven-day mandatory
        overtime to
    the unemployment line.
The workers were hammered and dazed.
    It came out of the blue.
From the heights to the pits.
From "We want you. You can't take a day off" to:
    "Get out, we are closing the plant down."
If you were lucky enough to hold a job –
    "We want concessions. Give us money back or hit the
        road."
They pitted local against local.
    "Livonia gave us a buck an hour. What'll you guys give."

The people turned to Japanese cars
and I can't blame them.

So you stood in the unemployment line.
Outside in the cold Michigan winter
with thousands of guys in line before you.
And Time magazine came and took pictures
of workers shuffling along,
forming a line blocks long.
Sullenly staring, with cigarettes dangling from
frigid lips.
And you pondered your future
(and the line snaking around a corner ahead of
you.)
"What went wrong?"
    "Did John Q. get fed up?"
"Evidently he did."
    "Along with Jane Q."
At this point all you wanted was
to grasp that green check in your numb hand and
grab a brew.
      In a warm place.

We put the world on wheels!
How could they do this to us?
Now hundreds of thousands of good, hard workers
are flipping hamburgers at minimum wage.
And I can't help but feel for them.

And now on the sunny Sunday afternoons
going to visit Grandma
    the numbers are still.
    They rest from Friday evening to Monday morning.
    The sign presents the same unmoving face to
    the dark of twilight and the sparse morning
commuters.

As we drive by I turn my head south
and look fixedly at the sign
    until we are past.
    So my wife and boys won't see
    the tears in my eyes.

■ ENDAKO SHUTDOWN
ANDREW WREGGITT

Now they wait
bunched in the hotel coffee shop
There is nothing to say,
the mine is closed and there is no work
Nothing to do but wait
Maybe in the new year

They were caught suddenly, incredulous
a breath stopped in mid-sentence
"This is dangerous," a man says
but even he is unsure of what he means
Dangerous for whom?
The millwrights, the mechanics, the drivers,
everyone had a certain power
to make wheels turn, to start a crusher
and make it work, feel the power in it,
in themselves
Now the mine is gone, inexplicable
the hands still reach out in dreams
for levers and tools
They wake confused, not understanding
After all these years
poured into the ground
the company owes nothing
What can you put back, if money
is not enough,
when there is nowhere else to go?

All around them the machines
have stopped, seized by economics
business a thousand miles away
Maybe in the new year, the company says
This is what they bring home to their families,
a piece of paper crumpled in a pocket

The man in the cafe repeats,
"This is dangerous,"
his huge hands around a coffee cup

But the sentence stops, incomplete
No one is sure what he means

■ THE WORK OF LOOKING FOR WORK
M.R. APPELL

the work of looking for work,
the drudgery of the work of looking for work,
i've had my fill of it,
do you understand?
i've had my fill of it.

walking around, taking the bus, driving
around looking for work
in the snow & the rain & the sun
& sitting in restaurants,
cigarettes & cups of coffee

mulling it all over in your mind:
trying to be confident,
trying to be imaginative,
trying to luck in
at being at the right place

at the right time.
signs in windows:
no help wanted.
read the help wanted ads in the paper:
aggressive, obnoxious

grab the world by the tail
salesman wanted
to sell new & used cars,
revolutionary new appliance,
or: not afraid to work long hours

for minimum wage
minimum satisfaction.
only the desperate need apply.
then too
it's all you can do sometimes

to get beyond these fashion plate
secretaries & receptionists
whose job it was you'd think
not to meet people or type letters
but to act as body guards

to the bosses
in oak panelled offices
behind them:

are you trying to be pushy, buddy?
now turn around & be on your way

or i'll open my desk drawer
& pull out my trusty Colt 45
& blast you into the street.
i can assure you
you won't land on your feet.

hell, even when i was fresh
right out of college
& ready to set the world on fire
i was six weeks,
six weeks driving around

in a suit & tie in the heat,
going from office to office
of construction firms,
engineering firms,
in Kitchener, Guelph, Cambridge,

trying to find work,
to apply my new found skills.
sorry but we require
at least two or three years experience.
also, in case you haven't noticed:

there is no pay for the work of looking for work.
the work of looking for work,
the drudgery of the work of looking for work,
i've had my fill of it,
do you understand?

■ NOBODY'S HEROES
M.R. Appell

three weeks unemployed
sitting at home
warm & comfortable
when i suddenly
out of the blue
get this job
out on a school roof
wet snow blowing
cold & thick
across the landscape
working with tar
& crushed stone
on a roofing crew
for just above
minimum wage.

come the end
of the day
we ride in the back
of the open truck
through the centre
of town
like battle weary soldiers
but there are no women & children
lining the streets
cheering & waving & throwing kisses
for we are nobody's heroes.

▌ GETTING IT UP
— it's not what you're thinking
M.R. Appell

i don't think anyone really understands
which already is an unfair statement
because i've never really told anyone
how i feel.
but again:
i don't think anyone really understands
what the years of unemployment,

the genuine layoffs,
the layoffs that thinly disguised
being fired by spineless bosses
& the years of obtaining a higher education
only to still be unemployed
have done to me.
no one sees or senses
the internal gut wrenching anxiety i experience,
the shaky nerves & the deep depression,
the lack of confidence
& the loss of the will to fight the system
or stand on my own.
i feel like an impotent man
wanting to make love
& unable to get it up;
easier to roll over
& go to sleep.

no
i don't think anyone really understands:
not my mother, my father,
my in-laws,
not Ginny lying in bed.
they don't see or sense the inner turmoil
as i get dressed at six in the morning
about to start yet another job,
to work with yet another group of people
(i find it hard to conceive
working at the same job, the same company,
with the same people
for thirty-five or forty years)
wondering which one will prove
to be the back stabber,
the credit stealer,
the lazy one i have to cover for
being new & all that,
the ass kisser
& the one who takes a disliking to me.
wondering too
if the happy-go-lucky boss
is really only a short sighted

narrow minded minor
tyrant in disguise.

no
i don't think anyone really understands
sees or senses
how sometimes
i just want to run,
to run away.
to run until i drop.
only going off
to this new job now
because it's expected of me
or because i hold out some thin hope
that all will go well
& the job will turn out to be a good one,
some inner & financial stability finally mine.

■ THE PANAMA CANAL
CLEM STARCK

My neighbour, an out-of-work welder,
is of the opinion that – well, you take for example
the Panama Canal...
"It was ours!" he keeps saying.
"It was built with our own sweat and blood!"

He would never have given it away
as our spineless President did.

All week it's been raining.
Jobs are scarce and he's been laid off.
However, he believes
the new President, a hard-liner,
will get this country back where it should be.

"Of course," he concedes
with a boyish grin, "there might be war."
But he doesn't think the Russians
will put up much of a fight.

While we talk, I can hear his wife
inside, vacuuming.

THE MYTH OF THE SELF-MADE MAN, or CASUALTIES, 1982

Zoë Landale

This is the way fishermen go down:
in ruins;
high-bowed boats padlocked to wharves,
sheriff's seals slammed against varnished doors.
Good fishermen, bad fishermen, their debts
are indifferent;
they speak a heritage of diminishing returns.
These men are nameless now,
they have no boats.
Dispossessed, they wake on windy nights
with the taste of rust, pull and clatter
of iron chains.

Their boats were arrival, were home;
devouring sweethearts, blunt and ambitious.
Too ambitious, or at the wrong time:
other fishermen, satisfied with
lesser craft,
don't owe so much money.
They still have keys, a familiar hull to gentle.

Sea-time has taught economy
of complaint, the futility
of curses.
Who can the men blame but
the times,
the banks, themselves?
All that weather for nothing, for years.
Sharp seas and
nausea of remorseless work;
off-shore grounds they know better
than the bodies of their wives.

Each man's loss is an anguish
known by everyone.
There ought to be a scorecard
in each harbour:
behind sympathy, relief breaks the surface

of neighbour's eyes:
Thank God it's not me.

Dread follows the men
like a history of rot.
One, two decades they've worked;
the bank may take it all.
Haven't fishermen paid taxes,
haven't they believed in success?
Always they thought only
bums
went bankrupt.
This is the way fishermen drown:
in debt,
hard men, bewildered
by a sudden failure of myth

▌ LAY OF THE LONG-LIVED LEFTOVERS, or
▌ UNEMPLOYED PLAINSONG
ZOË LANDALE

These days I spend my time
trying to use up leftovers.
Whatever I do, wash dishes,
water plants, conservation
gnaws a substratum to thought
manic   unsatisfying
as skim milk.
Tonight we'll have diced ham
with noodles and cheese, enough for
2 meals.
That still leaves enough chopped ham
for another dinner.
Ham gougère, perhaps,
avec champignons, or –
            There are more noodles, too,
labelled, wrapped and deposited
in the freezer.
Last night was turkey
again,
masked in white sauce with
thyme, tarragon, rosemary, curry,

wrapped in a crusty biscuit roll.
Our friends loved it.
What was left over, I heated
for lunch.
　　　　Still blessing the freezer
is more turkey.

I lust after recipes
like a fat woman after fudge
ice cream;
malice aforethought or
economy.
Leftovers, JOY OF COOKING seduces
in bacon
breads, cakes and crackers
noodle dish
potatoes　　　see also
Brunch, Lunch and Supper Dishes.
Efforts crescendo.
Food is sauced, spiced, cheesed,
rolled, bludgeoned:
I am merciless!
War on waste!
Festoon your kitchen with washed
and drying plastic bags.

Hope in your freezer,
keep your marking pen alert
for scraps.
To your mixing bowls, cooks!
Believe in eggs.
Garlic saves.
　　And
　　　　　gratification:
in November we achieve our
all-time low food bill for a month,
3 cats
2 people
$197.16
　　　　　My husband calls me
Queen of the Leftovers.

The Queen accepts the accolades of
satisfied followers with becoming
humility.
She is already consumed
already plotting dinner
it's infinitely reusable

■ MEA CULPA
ZOË LANDALE

These days even the kitchen
has been secularized.
Vegetables are served with
lashings
of psychology.
Meal-time conversation shatters
like the wineglasses
she hurled against a wall.
Always, there is too much
vinegar   in the salad.
Bills they cannot
pay
shock like worms   in an apple's flesh.
They are ashamed
of small repairs left undone;
evasions of dinner out
with friends. Explanations:
there is nothing more he can do.
While she probes possibilities
like an obsessed dentist,
he, the culprit,
paints a sign over each eye.
One reads
out of work. The other
mea culpa.
He does not sit long
in his chair after dinner.
If he did, she might sweep him up with the
glittering fragments of their
rage
and throw him out the door

■ LOTTERIES
JAMIE PEARSON

At four in the morning
I wake my wife to tell her
there's an ad in the classifieds.
First one in a week, I tell her, but
she tells me, she has to be up
in two hours.
So I go back to my paper
and begin to fabricate a new resume
changing a few lines and dates
hoping to hide the time
attempting to regain what I have lost
I tell my wife as she drags herself
to the bathroom still not fully awake.
I put my clothes on,
hunt for a stamp and walk out the door,
dropping my application into the mail
box on the corner,
feeling a part of myself falling
off into the darkness with my letter
mixed in with a pile of white envelopes
on a desk begging for the time
to be read. I stop at the store
and buy a lottery ticket.

■ JOB PLACEMENT BOARD
PAM TRANFIELD

Dogfish
Cleaners and Cutters
$5 hour for cleaners and cutters and 10 cents for fish
skinners. 40 hour week. You must have
at least 1 month experience
skinning, cleaning, or cutting dogfish.

Gallery Helper
This art gallery requires a person
to mount Chinese painting,
and if they are or need a paint touch up do it.
They will also carve your name in Chinese letters on stamps so

that you can stamp your name on something.
Will do other j
obs when not needed. This person does not have to
speak English.

DEAR FOREMAN...
Production of Goods

■ STEEL EDGES
Calvin Wharton

When the afternoon shift
shut down last night
someone left the sawmill
the toes of his right foot
      caught in a roller
      and no steel-toed boots;

The sawmill is a dangerous place,
even foremen are susceptible:
      Alex, who should have known better,
      jumped from a catwalk
      to the cant deck, below,
      missed
      and shattered his knee
      on the hard steel lip
      of a conveyer belt;

Encouragement from lunchroom safety posters
doesn't seem to help;

Once, at the trimsaw,
an over-length two-by-four
I couldn't get around or under,
knocked me into the bin
where a saw blade buzzed
inches from my face
until the sorter operator noticed
and turned off the power;

And every week
I pick up new bruises,
a blackened fingernail,
or slightly-sprained thumb . . .

Saturday night
in the Billy Barker Hotel,
I drink beer with other millworkers,
listen to their gruesome stories

told as if pain and mutilation
were a glorious tradition,

Yes, we all know the sound
of one hand clapping
down at the sawmill.

■ THE HORN BLOW
JEFF TAGAMI

All day pounding nails
with an air hammer
the sound as loud as a gun,
I can hardly hear Franky singing
some nonsense lullaby.
Today, it's pig gates
and the boss wants 400
before the rains come down.
Forklift drops another unit
of wood, we pop in a cartridge
of two-inchers and start shooting.
When the oil smoke
clears, I see it is Franky who coughs
and coughs until his black
tongue hangs out and sawdust
settles like snow
on his moustache.
Beyond our table
the sawmen are busy
watching out for what fingers
they have left. Above their heads
they hang crosses, a rubber duck,
blond dolls.
If not for luck, then to pray
against a spastic knee
that brings the spinning blade
down like an axe
sending fingers or a whole hand
flying to heaven.
To daydream is to lose a part of you.
Ask Blanquet's three severed
fingers, ask Franky, the crazy one,

who will hide his hand in his sleeve
and hold it before you to shake.
And it is his hands
cracked and raw
that never heal.
Shotgunned stomach. One-kidney-Franky.
One hot day he revealed
that stomach to me, slowly raising
his T-shirt, and proclaimed
it the Map of California.
I saw the deadened nerves,
I saw the network of blue veins
leading to nowhere,
or here, his ramshackle house
leaning on its bad foundation
behind this lumberyard of new wood.
I knew then
it was a map of all the places
he's never been,
and if there were names of cities,
he could neither read
nor write them.
I knew nothing could kill him,
not even himself.
Now he faces me across the work table
in his one grey jacket, grease
stained and too thin
to be of any use.
He is picking at a splinter
lodged deep in his palm
like a new vein
and throbbing.
He looks up at the clouds,
calls the rain
to come down, You, Mother.
But it doesn't.
We work until muscles grow
even in our fingers.
When the horn goes off
signalling the end of work,
it is Franky who turns
to me with the wisdom

of all his 29 years
and says, "The horn blow!"
So I follow him, stumbling
through the nail strewn path
with no questions asked
past the stacked bins and pallets
because the horn blow.
Out the gate
through the darkness
we head for home
before the flood lights
blink on and the saws grind
to a stop
baring their crooked grins.

■ **from FACTORY: II**
  ANTLER

"All you have to do is stand here
          and package lids as they come from the press
          checking for defects every so often.
Shove enough lids in the bag like this,
Stand the filled bag on end like this,
Fold over the top like this,
Pull enough tape off
          and tape it like this,
Then stack 'em like this on the skid."

How many watching me watch the woman
          teach me my job
Remembered *their* first day on the job,
Remembered wondering what the woman felt
          teaching them in a minute
          the work she'd done all her life,
Showing them so fast all they needed to know?
How many could still remember who they were in search of a living –
Name, address, telephone, age, sex, race,
Single, married, children, parents, what they do or why they died,
Health record, police record, military record, social security #,
          how far in school, everywhere worked, why quit or fired,
          everything written here is true, signature, interview,
          the long wait, the call "you're hired" –

Could still see themselves led through the factory
          to the spot they would work on,
          strange then and now so familiar?

This is the hall big as a football field.
Here are the 24 presses chewing can lids
          from hand-fed sheets of aluminum.
Here are the 10 minsters chomping poptops
          nonstop into lids scooped into their jaws.
Machines large as locomotives,
          louder than loudest rockgroup explosions,
Screeching so loud you go deaf without earplugs,
          where the only way to speak is to gesture,
Or bending to your ear as if I were telling a secret
          the yell from my cupped hands less than a whisper.

Now the film of myself each day on the job begins.
I see myself enter the factory, led to the spot I will work on.
I see myself adjusting the earplugs to stopper the deluge of sound.
I see the woman who showed me the job
          she'd done her whole life in a minute
Let me take over, and the minute she left how I fumbled,
          how the lids gushed all over the floor
And when the foreman rushed over and I hollered –
          "Something's wrong! It's too fast!
          No one can work at this speed!"
How he stared and the stares of the others
          who couldn't hear what I said but could tell.
And I gulped, This "Beat the Clock" stunt
          must be performed *eight hours*
          before the lunatic buzzer itself
          becomes consolation prize.

Yet sooner than I thought, I mastered the rhythms,
          turned myself into a flywheel dervish,
And can't deny being thrilled by the breakthrough
          from clumsy to graceful –
Though old-timers scowled as if it took years
          to learn all the fine points.
But long after my pride in doing such a good job
          turned into days crossed off the calendar
          each night before pulling out the alarm

I woke to push in,
up, eat, go, work, eat, work, back, eat, sleep,
All the days I would work stared
ahead of me the line of machines,
behind me the line of machines,
Each with a worker working as I work,
doing the same job that I do,
Working within sight of the wall clock
whose second hand is still moving.

■ **from FACTORY: IV**
ANTLER

All I have to do is stand here
and do the same thing all day.
But the job requiring five steps repeated over and over
eight hours every day
is not monotonous.
Only the body and mind finding such work monotonous
is monotonous.
Those who gripe work is boring
gripe they are boring.

Yet if I work hours and the clock says
only five minutes has gone by,
If the last hour working seems longer
than the seven before it,
Won't my last day on the job seem longer
than all the months that preceded it?
Could I have been here more in one day
than someone who's put in ten years?
Or has he learned how to punch in and out
fast as a punching bag?
Don't we both know the way
to the prong of our alarm in the dark?
How long could I work without looking up at the clock?
How long before I was watching its hands
more than watching my own package lids?

It's not so terrible that every second dies
or that whatever I am every second dies
or that what we call death

is death only of the final second,
But it is terrible (not like movies that lead us
        down corridors to doors springing slimy
            buffooneries) –
Terrible as having to eat meat killed in factories is terrible,
        as having to wear clothes made in factories is terrible,
        as having to live in homes built by strangers
            and exist among millions of strangers
        and be born and buried by strangers is terrible,
Too terrible for terrible to have any meaning –
        that every second dies
            whoever I could possibly be.

■ THE COIL WINDER
Sue Doro

Beatrice the coil winder
brushes her teeth ten times a day

management does not care
because Beatrice winds coils
faster than anyone ever hired
for the job

Beatrice swallows pills
almost as often as she brushes her teeth

she's grateful for the job
management has given her

she winds coils faster and faster

brushes her teeth more and more

swallows her valiums and methedrines
with tranquil speed

and talks to no one

Beatrice the coil winder
doesn't remember how

■ EARL'S POEMS: 1 and 3
SUE DORO

1
on a good day
Earl runs the lathe next to me

spins those train axles in ol' number seven
     with ease

cuts coils of shiny blue metal chips
like little fat slinky spring toys

makes number seven hummmmmmmmmm with
     delight
when he's on a roll

then in late afternoon
he'll slow down the day

put another axle in the machine
turn it on
and "cut air"
while he reads the sports page

'cause Earl – he'll NEVER NEVER bust
     the rate

3
Earl broke me in on number eight
     journal lathe
a fifteen foot long sucker of a machine
that cuts the parts of train axles
that stick out from the wheels

one and a half tons of trouble
spinning around in a blur
looks like a giant's weightlifting dumbbells
I mean
the whole damn thing gets put into the lathe

and Earl, he shows me what to do
he says: "no woman ever ran this job before
don't worry you'll do just fine"
says to take my time...be safe
don't worry 'bout production
then Earl...he's so calm...so calm
he made even MY nerves relax
and he was right
in time...I did just fine

▌YOU CAN'T GO BACK TO WORK IN THE MIDDLE OF A CARD GAME
SUE DORO

playing poker
for dimes
at lunchtime
in the wheel shop

we are low-key
competition players
coins changing hands
as quick as a clock's tick

no cut-throat here
we laugh
yell
swear
slap cards on the table

and finish one last fast game
right into the blast
of the noon whistle

■ DORIS'S POEM
SUE DORO

Allis Chalmers Tractor Shop

the machine she runs
is a washer as big as a semi-trailer
no clothes go in it

hot chemical water
fumes from its dark openings
at both ends

a conveyer belt travels through it
on first shift it takes two workers
to tend the washer

on second for the last 20 years
there's Doris

she loads one end
with 15 or 20
tractor engine parts
each steel piece
weighing an average
of 25 pounds

she walks around to the other side
waiting for them to emerge
hot and steamy
like boiled steel cabbages

she sprays the remaining dirt and chips
blowing in their bolt holes
with a high pressure air hose

the hose tries to pull from her
        gloved hand
like an electric eel

she won't let it
she has control

she's Doris on the washer

Doris could retire in 2 years
but she doesn't plan to

she thinks she'll work

as long as they let her

she has 2 kids at home
teenagers . . . you know how they eat

she just saved enough for a down payment
on a house
she's always wanted to go to California
to visit her oldest daughter

she won't retire yet

Doris lights a cigarette
it's 8 p.m.
second shift lunchtime
sweat shines on her forehead
her grey hair is wet with it

she wipes her face
with a clean shop rag
she puffs her cigarette
sitting at the lunch table
in the women's locker room
an empty tuna can
is her ash tray

she comments on the heat
of the summer night
the stupid foreman
and the amount of work
she's NOT going to do

it's her strength
it's her strength
that I need to learn

it's her strength

■ FACTORY EDUCATION
JIM DANIELS

Bobbie Joe eyes me
sweating behind the parts washer,
tossing the parts into baskets.
He idles over from his broken machine
his pot sticking out tight
under a white t-shirt
grey hair slicked back perfect.

He bends over toward me
whiskey on his breath
and stares at my greasy coveralls:
"Hey, you don't have to get dirty
on this job. Look at me.
Am I dirty?
Am I sweating?
Look, you got to learn how to survive
around here, buddy.
If you don't know how to break your machine
then you shouldn't be runnin' it."
He wanders off, shaking his head.

I slide my earphones back on
and push my safety glasses up my nose.
The parts start piling up in front of me
so I toss them sloppy in the baskets,
pausing to straighten them into rows,
getting behind.

I see a part gliding crooked down the conveyor
and rush to straighten it
but catch myself.
The part gets caught on the washer's inside edge.
The conveyor chain clicks,
the parts piling up behind the jammed piece.

I turn my back
and stare at the big overhead crane
carrying a load of steel over my head,
honking its horn.

I snap my fingers, snap snap snap
until I hear the Big Snap
and turn back toward my machine,
press the stop button.
The chain, like a fried snake
lies bunched up behind the parts.

Bobbie Joe walks by and smiles,
patting his belly.
The foreman runs up cursing.
"Wasn't my fault. The part was crooked,"
I shout, pointing up the line.
He nods, "I'll get a mechanic over here right away."
I nod back, trying to remember
if I have any white t-shirts.

■ TIMERS
JIM DANIELS

A man with a stopwatch stares
at my hands, his thumb on the button.
He is timing how long it takes me
to take this part, put it in my machine,
push two buttons, take it out.

He is trying to eliminate my job.
But I take a second or two
to scratch my balls.
Got to allow time for that,
I wink at him.

He shakes his head,
his bright orange earplugs
wedged in tight.

I guess finally it's not him
who decides. He seems reluctant
to meet my eyes, jotting quick notes
in the aisle.

mebody somewhere's got a watch
on him too. Somebody's put us both here
where we can't hear each other.

■ SIGNING
JIM DANIELS

lunch: *open and close your mouth. Put your hand in front of it.*
Rapidly open and close the hand.

need paint: *slap paint across your face with a big brush*

need hi-lo: *steer a steering wheel*

break: *snap an arm in two*

need banjo housing: *strum one*

need housing covers: *draw a circle around your head*

need cigarette or joint: *fingers to lips*

need drink: *thumb in air, fingers in fist, raised to lips*

need welding sticks: *play drums*

need overhead crane: *point to rafters, twirl finger*

faster: *finger twirling in circle*

slower: *hands pushing down*

no: *you know that one*

no way: *point to crotch*

foreman coming: *tighten a tie*

machine broke down: *point to machine, thumbs down*

disgust: *wave hand down and away*

fuck you: *you know that one*

■ KILLBUCK: A POEM FOR GRINDERS
RICHARD STANSBERGER

I

Spitting orange seeds off the loading dock
old Killbuck said:
People ask me if I'm an alcoholic
and I just say
Whyno.

II

Killbuck stands in a cloud of dust
pressing a steel cylinder to the
screaming stone wheel.
Sweat streaks his face mask.
Sparks pit his leather apron.

III

Back in 1947 while playing ball
Killbuck noticed he couldn't close his hands.
He showed the plant nurse.
– When did it happen.
   Who are your witnesses.
– Twenty years as a goddam grinder,
   that's when it happened.
– I'm sorry but I need a specific time and place
   and a specific witness or witnesses
   or I can't turn it in for compensation.

IV

Things I learned from him:
how to shell a boiled egg with a spoon,
how to build a hammock out of crate sides,
when to sneak off and sleep in it,
how to goose guys with the air hose,
how to tell the age of a chainman
      (count his missing fingers),
where to hide the bottle.

■ THE SOUND: FACTORY SYSTEM POEM
Tom Wayman

The moment the hooter goes
I reach for the small cardboard case in my tool box
and tear off a tuft of cotton
to plug in each ear.

Before the shift starts,
in the low sounds of people clocking in,
getting changed and standing around drinking coffee
and talking, or reading the paper, the first aid man
puts a dozen new packages of ear cotton
on a table in his room
for anybody who has run out.

If I don't use it, the noise
doesn't seem so bad at the start
with rivets being hammered, the hiss of
air hoses, the shouts, engines, the pounding.
Yet as the first hours pass, the sound
begins to echo in my ear:
never deafening
but a steady high-pitched drilling
I'm always aware of.

                              Even with the cotton
I touch my ear to make sure the plugs are in place
when a router or winch seems especially loud.
The fibre
itches a little constantly
but if I take it out for a second
when I put the cotton back it's like on a hot day
when you dive under the surface of a sunlit lake
into the cool and quiet.

                              Speech
is audible almost unchanged:
people making suggestions, or jokes,
and what the foreman says to do next.
Occasionally I have to ask someone to talk louder, though.
A few guys wear Mickey Mouse ears – the headphones

which function the same as cotton.
But since the Company doesn't provide these
most of us stick with what we're given.

Yet if they could make an ear protector
so powerful that when we wore it
there was absolute silence,
a voice
would still speak continually here in the din
saying:

> a factory is not a tool
for production, like a screwdriver
or the compressed air impact wrench.
It is a way of organizing people
to do a job, human beings
who are supposed to follow orders
and not argue, perform
and not comment. There can be no such thing as
a socialist factory
any more than a left-wing, interest-charging bank
or a Red army. These structures, hierarchies
belong to another age
and have to be altered, dismantled, rebuilt
to improve them
for as along as they can't be shut down.
But they will never
be ours.

■ WALKING PAPERS
ANDREW WREGGITT

In the factory
all of us huddled around the time clock
the young boys grinning
and clutching time cards
Too young for legal-age
compensation, cash on the table
Faces black
grinning their white teeth
through the sweat and smudge
of metal dust

And when one falls
beneath a forklift
turning his hurt face
with tears against the floor
you say, too young for this
bullshit, all of it
You stand there with your time card
and say you want your money
your walking papers

And later they are in the bar
their young faces, grinning
believing this is just what happens
that there is no blame
You drink your beer
knowing you wanted something else
more than money, your freedom
You wanted a company
with a face to punch

■ **GOD HELPS THOSE**
   JEFF PONIEWAZ

After broiling all day
in the break-ass factory
I'm buried in a busload
of armpits remembering
the glowing letter the Company sent
accepting me for summer employment
and welcoming me to the Free
Enterprise System.
Suddenly the bus, which has already
been moving like a choked turd,
grunts to a dead stop.
I look out the window to see
a bridge going up.
Some asshole in an admiral's outfit
and with a mast just high enough
to stop traffic, opens what looks like
a cold can of beer
and his wife throws kisses at cars
which bleat like frantic ovens.

■ A-7 CRIB

LEON E. CHAMBERLAIN

I trudge to the door
on an arctic winter morning.
Before I enter or even get the door fully open
it leaps out
blasting me backward
like a howling, vindictive wind.

It springs out like a hungry animal and engulfs me
covering me from head to frigid foot
with its ear-numbing cacophony &
sinus-infecting smell.

Cutting machines howl as banshees are
released from the cold, hard steel.
Air hisses from a thousand pinholes.
Electric motors & hydraulic pumps
contribute their high-pitched whine to the din.

Hi-los dump their weighty loads.

Myriad parts tumble from chutes to thud into rusty
stock tubs with all the tranquillity of a bass drum.

I'm forced to shout to communicate
and after a while the oily mist
& yelling begin to take their toll
on my tortured throat and it
burns.

The noise wears you down.
It removes the protective sheathing
protecting your nerves &
robs you of your strength & patience.

It wears you plumb out
even if you only sit there
& never open your tool box
all day long.

At day's end you are weary
used up and spent.

The cumulative effects of it
grow worse each day & month & year.
It saturates your system
filling you as an hourglass is filled with sand.
It gets to you quicker each morning
until you just want to shriek &
seek blessed silence.

■ VISIONS
Leon E. Chamberlain

We enter the parking lot in pitch darkness...
driving single file, playing follow the leader...
snaking around the curves and snowbanks...
like lemmings headed for the sea...

but...our shimmering sea is the factory.

I think back...
        to elementary school...
where we would stand up and proclaim
        proudly what we wanted to be when we grew up.
Reveal our chosen profession. The thing we wanted to
                do for the rest of

                        our lives . . . . . .

The usual, well-known occupations were parroted...
For the girls – nurses or teachers or airline stewardess.
For us boys – fireman or cop or detective (from the admirers
of Boston Blackie.)

I never once heard a kid stand up and say:

"I want to be a scarifier operator, or
a left-hand vertical mill operator, or
        a number three cleaner, or
            a furnace job setter, or
                even the plant manager."

Thru the darkness . . . . . .
   I can see myself, plainly
   a typical, skinny, unconfident child
   of ten years old
   at Hall School
   flannel shirted and jeaned

stand up

and holding text book in quavering hand . . .
   proudly say . . .
     "I want to be a plumber-pipefitter.

And do neat things like
fix pipes. And install piping.

   Good pipes, ones that enable harried, harassed, rushed
people on the assembly line to get a cool drink of water or
meet simple human dignity by answering their bodily
functions. And . . .

I'll do steam fitting, working with dangerous high pressure
steam. To
   heat our plant and us and heat water to wash parts
   and wash ourselves. And

I'll work with my hands
     in the dirt
       installing plumbing
         to code with the proper pitch
           to get rid of our waste. And

I'll read blueprints and do pneumatic work
   on cylinders that speed parts along their path
     or twirl chucks holding gears, so
       the keen cutting tools can shape them. And

I'll lay out and erect huge pipes
   high in the steel
     that will convey

condensate and oils and
potable drinking water and
deadly chemicals safely thru the shop."

The vision abruptly fades...
as I park my Pinto...
among dozens of similarly jockeying cars...

   And I trudge in...
   blowing clouds of vapour in the frigid air. And
avoiding patches of ice hiding under the snow. And
traversing mounds of snow

that mark the boundaries between the rows of fluffy, white
vehicles.

               And I reflect . . . . . .

   "If I went back to ten years old...
      and stood before the class...
         at Hall school...

THAT'S WHAT I'd say."

I enter the gate.

The hell I would.

■ SONG, ENDAKO
Andrew Wreggitt

All the young men thrown from cars,
the bad boys drunk outside dance halls
Small town girlfriends
snuggled up close in the front seat
and only the black night highway
to pull apart finally
with the song of cylinders
and gasoline

The trip to the mine made
once too often

Raymond kept his foot on the gas pedal
left the ridge
and rose like a phoenix over the forest,
the trees singed and broken
in the fire of his loathing
His need, a spark struck against
the idiocy of everything,
the days gone mad with booze and work

Still the ore in the mine pulls
from the shovel's claw, tires howl
on the road that hugs
the torn mountain ridge

In the forest
the smell of burnt rubber mingles
with the sulphur from the mine stack
Bad boys drunk on the highway

Everyone here sings
to the stroke of engines

■ DEAR FOREMAN
JOHN MORTON

I blew out the Booster Fan
and did the legs
I cleaned the plugged hoppers
over 3-screw
I changed the bin-flows
on the Fuller-Kenyon pump
I lanced the slope on B-Fan
I rapped the Alleviator
and shovelled two luggers of dust
and I even washed down
the Economizer floor

so just
get off my back

■ SLIME WARNING
JOHN MORTON

The alarm bell
pulls me
grumbling from my daydream.

The control operator
must get up to press
the override button
and restore the peace
such as it is
in the Furnace Control Room:

the Top 40 repeating
itself endlessly
over quiet thunder.

The alarm bell again.
Get up.
Push the button.

The operator curses.
He always says
he should have a long stick
to push the button from his chair.
        (But there are limits
        in the Furnace Control Room.)

It is only
the slimes tank
overflowing.

■ BOILER LANCER
JOHN MORTON

It's three o'clock.
I can't tell night from day
but it doesn't matter
in the lancers' shack.

There was a time
lancers went out with banners and bugles
to face the enemy.
But this is 1981;
my lance an air-pipe hissing
and my banner a paycheque
every other Thursday
and I can't hear bugles
  (or anything else,
   through my earplugs)

as I drive my lance rapping
across the flaming rows of tubes
like cleaning pipes on some encrusted organ
within the doors of #2 Slag Boiler.
And my enemy?
  (I think about that
  sometimes
  when I am not lancing.)

The other lancers sleep.
My red eyes sweep the floor
and drill into the door
across the room, the one
that you can see was painted
orange before it was blue
and green before it was orange.

It has a ragged scar
where a thousand careless
angry lancer boots have kicked
their way out of this disgusting
shack full of idle bullshit
and old newspapers.

It's three o'clock
we've read it all
and said it all
  (I think about the enemy
  but he is not here)

In a few hours
I'll go home
to the world.

■ PIN-BOY
JOHN MORTON

midnight coffee flows
like water
in the Furnace Control Room

we read
scraps of newspaper to the
dull synthetic excitement
of the radio

but when we go out to tap the furnace
the plug shatters in a golden shower
the slag runs
we are alive

a new plug in place
the operator fires me upstairs
with a lifted hand
to the door that says:
"Caution: Crane Charging"

now I am alert and fully
aware of thunder
poison fume of the great pots moving
bright fury in the night

I am the Furnace Helper
ready
as a cauldron of molten slag
comes to hover over my head

darting
out to drive home the pin

watching
for the unexpected

as the glowing gold is tipped
into the raging furnace

I am Pin-Boy
who charges the furnace

I am an animal
poised
on the balls of my feet

■ THE SINTERING PLANT
JOHN MORTON

hard to believe
it was supposed to be
a white-shirt-and-tie operation

and now they say,
sure, you can wear a white shirt
in there if you want to...

there's a certain change
happens to everything
that is built here:
the best laid plans go
haywire, the slime & rust
the dusts & foul gases
do their work on the clean ideas
of engineers & planners

  and on the minds
  of working men

  message scratched
  in the flaky black coating
  of a huge pipe:

LICK ME

■ GRAVEYARD SHIFT
PETER TROWER

I am walking through Alcan's inferno
with Luigi Milanas
expatriate ex-paratrooper
at 4:30 in the glum
potline morning
sucking scorched air
down aisles of popping flame
only our millwright coveralls
distinguishing us
from the grubby goblins
in thick brown pants without pockets
who tend to their functions and fires
making aluminum   bad lungs   money
by luciferian light.

The cranes crash past above us
carrying snouted crucibles
to suck the magma from the pits
like ants from a hill –
Men ride three-wheeled crustbreakers
to rattling battle,
lashing airhose tails
they peck at the pot-edges like birds –
Greasy yellow lift-trucks
clatter through the ruckus
driven on sullen errands
by Germans who still mourn Hitler –
buzzers   sweat   salt-tablets –
goggles   face-masks   the taste of smoke –
I dream of the roasting voltage
pumping like blood through transformers
into these alchemic halls
to powerdance through the cathodes
cooking the bauxite silver
the careless-black
and the careless black of Sally's hair
and black-label beer . . .
I fall asleep on my feet
and walk into a wall.

It's our once-nightly tour of duty
After this, if all is well
we can doze in the orangepeel lunchrooms –
drink robot soup and cocoa –
thumb through dogeared skinbooks
till punchout time   But not tonight because

a crane has broken down
at the south end of Line 2.

"Let's go," says Luigi, sadly.

■ IN TOTO
TIMOTHY RUSSELL

A man I knew was killed one day at work,
burned in a freak shower of molten slag
that caught him bent at a water fountain,
as if he were clerk instead of welder,
so somehow safe from death at thirty-nine.
The accident took place on daylight turn.

News of it hit, starting afternoon turn,
and lingered with me, affecting my work,
the evening Bob died, barely thirty-nine
years old, burnt, as I shovelled other slag
and thought. Half his life he was a welder,
twenty years, then at a water fountain

when thick, orange-hot slag found the fountain,
he died, surprised he had to take his turn.
Did some greater foreman need a welder?
I never talked to Bob, except at work,
never saw him outside the mill, where slag
washed over him when he was thirty-nine.

I should not care that he was thirty-nine
or that he died at a water fountain
suffering that sudden hot splash of slag
perhaps, but should about his urge to turn
in that awful heat to return to work
where he would not be victim, but welder,

215

for his survival was as a welder,
and had nothing to do with thirty-nine.
And it could be another day at work,
and he could avoid the water fountain.
Yes, I should care about his urge to turn
back to his job despite the bath of slag,

his last gesture, made despite glowing slag.
If I do not remember this welder,
or what I shovelled on afternoon turn,
whenever I encounter thirty-nine,
let me drink from that same water fountain.
I have an idea that it will work.

Wherever I work there is always slag,
sometimes a fountain, sometimes a welder,
sometimes thirty-nine lines that will not turn.

■ **WIRED RAW**
JEFF FRIEDMAN

The noise was immense
like two oceans in my ears
but I wore no earplugs, so I could hear
a skip in the machine, a break
in its cutting rhythm.

Bending down over and over
I scooped hot wires, rods
not yet baked with flux,
from a metal gut
and rolled them evenly into a bin.

The machine operator, sitting
in a sound-proof room,
read his novel
and watched me through glass
while the giant spool hammered

against cement as it unravelled
feeding wire through the cutter.
For a second when I stood up straight

and saw late afternoon sun
hitting the windows high above me,

clusters of dust like seeds
blown from the heads of dandelions,
I thought of the light that swam lazily
in the machine operator's goggle lenses.
I thought of the foreman with his broad face

and pointed ears like a German Shepherd's
how one year ago he removed me from the packing line
and gave me this pair of heavy leather gloves.
When the gut cramped with wire –
the rhythm of the cutter growing bumpy –

I let it go – signalled no one –
and a second later dove behind a bin
to duck the rods
shooting all over the place
like someone else's problems.

■ ASBESTOS
SUSAN EISENBERG

Floating like
            snowflakes it
flutters
      and sways as it
clings to your clothes and your hair and
            it tingles
            it tickles
            it swells up your throat
until every breath becomes itchy and tight.

Like a sweater you swallowed
it rubs up inside you and nudges and
scrapes against tracheal tissue.
                        It slips
through the bronchi and into
                        your lungs
where it burrows and giggles and scratches

and tugs until – who
                    would suspect
that those drifting white
featherflakes floating through
schools and through hospitals, factories –
hairdryers! – who would suspect them?

and why weren't we told
        way back in the thirties
of the cancerous findings that
never were published, but financed and
buried by the burgeoning industry –
cancerous findings! conclusively proven
back in the thirties –

and now so much later,
still we're installing asbestos
asbestos   you die so much later,
20 years later you die from those snow-
feather particles
                    drifting throughout the city:
protecting the wires, protecting the ducts,
protecting the products
                    packaged
to kill you.

▌ CHOICE CUT-UP CHICKEN (1962) LTD.
▌ or HOW I SPENT MY SUMMER VACATION
DAVID EVEREST

"You'll start out washing crates"
recently emptied
their occupants already dead
"Pile them here
try to keep your mouth closed."

After two days of water and chickenshit
one of the hangers got sick
and I went on the line.
Four hangers working in a cage
rip open a crate
grab a flapping chicken

jam its legs in the loops moving past my face
go for another one
until the crate moves out of reach
and another started.

I worked various other jobs
on the line that summer
following the line of hung chickens
as they were in turn
stuck by the killers
bled (pet food)
then the plucking machines
after that gutted
then the disassembly line:
dismembered and iced in bushel baskets
labelled
legs
   breasts
wings
   backsanecks.

As a high school student
I didn't need (and wasn't offered)
the privilege of overtime
(getting up at two a.m.
take a truck out to pick up a load)
like Maclean
(only a year older than me
but with a young family)
who tipped the truck his first night
on some back road
and spent the rest of the night chasing chickens
frantically

so he wouldn't be late for work.

Not many people knew
unless somebody told them
that Frank
working near the plucking machines
was yodelling all day
   at the top of his lungs.

It was quieter in the cold room
it was cool
and it didn't smell like anything
but a fridge full of a few tons of raw chicken.

Later in the summer I was spending
most of my time in the cold room
making up orders for supermarkets
and loading trucks
interrupted
from time to time
by the cry "more bad backs"
when I would stand
paintscraper at the ready
watching for chickens passing
with a crusty yellow growth on their backs
which I would remove
giving them the proper
chicken-skin-white back
usually somewhat lacerated.

I spent about two months there
at a cent and a half a minute
and never did see the people
who controlled the speed of the line
so that
at the end of eight hours
all the chickens that had been sold
had also been shipped
and iced
and taken apart
and gutted
plucked
stuck
hung
unloaded from the trucks
which had brought them
from their broiler houses
where they had lived
since they had been hatched.

■ HOW TO DRESS A SALMON
MICHAEL B. TURNER

Pre-graded, right?
No pew marks, seal bites,
net marks, back breaks?
Okay.
Now put the knife in.
Here.
Good.
Just the tip.
Take the tail.
Right.
Now push-pull it.
Stop.
Flip it.
Good.
Now pass it on.

Pulling the gill.
Now you can use more knife.
Here.
Turn the head, not the blade.
Good.
Now where's the gill?
Comes off like a ring, right?
Good.
Now pass it on.

Reaming it.
You have to cut the membrane.
See.
Cut that.
Good.
Now you rip.
Hear that pop?
Okay.
Good.
Now leave it for the washers.

■ THE WASHERS'LL WASH IT

MICHAEL B. TURNER

There's ten of 'em.
Real young.
All from the canning lines.
They're here 'cause their work's too slow.
They drive the older women crazy.

But I get 'em working.
Out here's too close.
Ev'ryone knows so and so.
And no one's slow.
Out here we go one speed.

■ 7:59 A.M.

MICHAEL B. TURNER

Company man stands on a tote
and thinks he's ten feet tall.
His watch extends long past the dock,
the parking lot, the hotels and motels
we wake up from.

He sees our kitchen tables.
And from our kitchen tables he sees us
flickering, grabbing for underwear,
wincing into clothes all wet with overtime.

As he drinks the coffee we don't have time for
he thinks a lot about our sleep, how we dream
of milts and roe, loose bones,
belly burn, pew holes . . .

Company man now tippy-toed, taller
as the time grows closer, plants a thought
beneath our heads: company clock's a moment slow.

In his eyes we know we're tardy
but stop to look and light a smoke.
He opens his mouth to bring us down.
The whistle blows, we punch in late.

■ RAT HOLE
CALVIN WHARTON

Beneath the street, a basement
jammed with printing artifacts
and uncountable, potentially usable items,
too many machines and containers,
shelves, and packages of paper;
too many boxes, boards, ceiling tiles,
broken chairs, and incomplete jobs.

In one corner, the light-table,
a sheet of frosted glass
lit from underneath,
centre of my work world
a universe slowly compressed
as projects encroach, constrict, threaten.

I sit in this windowless rat hole,
construct what will become print,
stare at the light shining up
through glass and paper
or regard crumbling plaster over brick walls,

where I pass the days
struggling for my daily cheese.

IN JULY/86 I GAVE NOTICE AT MY PROOFREADING JOB IN TORONTO, BECAUSE I HAD BEEN INVITED TO "SPLIT SHIFT," THE FIRST WORK WRITING CONFERENCE, AUGUST 21–24, IN VANCOUVER
PHIL HALL

When the clear plastic overlay
of this two-colour coupon is lifted

the bullets prices and logos
that will get printed red

seem to hover
above the base blue copy –

effortless clouds above the prairies
are hovering also this morning

their shadows unconnected below
on those hard-won patchworks of ground –

Proofread these coupons another month
then settle back in a window seat

and look down – as now
as always – for flaws

■ HERRING SEASON
David Conn

The wharves are empty.
The herring fleet is out,
loading on the Plimsoll
between profit and disaster:
a hold full of fish.

Spring reveals a horizon
at last, but onshore,
arc flashes overshadow day.
Here, welders go through
the motions of production

in a fitting shop dimmed
by chemical smoke.
As next year's boats take shape
between light-blasted walls,
the fragrant season passes.

■ WELDERS' TIME
David Conn

Inside the cage
of steel framing
becoming a ship,
time crawls at
two meters per hour –
a worm of molten rod

prodded along
a deck seam.

■ SOME KIND OF BONUS
DAVID CONN

It might be the spring:
no other reason to find
tranquillity in the act
of tossing scrap metal
into a steel bin.

The fitters have been busy
gutting the fishboat above.
I relay the burnt, rusted
entrails for recycling.

Unaccustomed quiet, the
silvery river carrying
occasional laden boats
in strengthening sun –

an aftermath. Today I
gain more than wages.

■ SONG OF THE HAMMER
DAVID CONN

Whatever can't be changed elsewhere,
here is the bending to the will.
We put the heating torch
to a buckled plate,
then sledge the steel.

From flimsy blueprints,
soon torn and burnt,
we build the sheer line
and compartments of a ship,
true to the trained eye.
Let those who can, tell us
how to do our job.

Let them give us a hammer big enough
(and stand back),
and we could reshape
this cold-bent coastline
to match the great bulwark
curve of our vessel,
blue horizon on black space.

■ FALSE CREEK
DAVID CONN

This ten minute break
means more than the last
two working hours,
being my own time.

I sit heavily on the wharf
and bathe my eyes in the city
reflections deep in False Creek.
Out there are the lights

of leisure, blinking and swarming.
The view is only a distraction
from work, until a harbour tug
eases in to pick up a barge.

Everything visible, but darkness
and water, is the product of
someone's work: a net of hours
snaring us all, day and night.

Darkness and water surround
the tug crew. Their work is
abetted by their breezy motion,
their independence.

We at the shop are pinned
in the floodlights, hobbled to
our machines. The tug's wake laps
the wharf. Past time to go inside.

CALLING YOU ON MY BREAK
Human Relations

■ CLASS CONSCIOUS
KATE BRAID

I put my hands on the table
right after you noticed the hammers
I wear for earrings.
An accidental gesture
        sort of.
The hands that wield a hammer
I wanted to show you
so there'd be no illusions
about me
        tough woman
        tough hands.
I didn't want you to get the wrong idea
about me
        looking so feminine in some parts.
What you see
my hands say for me
is what you get.

I put my hands on the table
tentative
proud   sort of
hoping you are one of the ones
who likes a working hand

and scared you're not.

■ MIDNIGHT DATE
JIM DANIELS

After calling you on my last break
I watch the sun set
over rolls of steel
rusting in the factory yard.

Old Green, the jobsetter, lies
on a piece of greasy cardboard
hands folded over his chest.
He opens his eyes and looks at me:
"Get a good education."

229

I close mine and see your shiny hair
falling across my face.
The foreman calls me back,
shoots me with a finger.

■

I put on earphones, safety glasses,
shove my hands into sweaty leather
and stand in dim light waiting
for axle housing tubes to rattle
down the line, to drop their grey weight
into my hands. I throw my head back
and howl your name: two more hours.
I kick my steel toes against steel.

■

Old Green gives the *break* sign.
I toss my gloves in a barrel,
punch my card, wash up.

I leave the locker room
with clean hands and step out
into what I want to believe
is a skyful of good will,
is a parking lot lined with possibility.

Tonight the moon looks full enough
to feed a lot of hearts. Mine rises
like the bird furthest from this factory.
Oh, tonight let's shed our clothes
and dance in this cool air.
Let's taste the moon's
clean white meat.

■ NIGHTWATCH
M.C. Warrior

staring into the radar
like a cat, i imagine
myself biting
the nape of your neck,

your throat, the arch
of an eyebrow

then walk out onto the dodger
to check the running lights
and distract myself
by timing the Sheringham light
as it winks lasciviously
at the American shore.

■ BILLY
LYN FERLO

Billy came through the office today.
EVERYONE was wishing they had worn a skirt.
We ran our fingers through our hair
and tried to keep our eyes
from running out of control
over his
fine
blue
denim.

It was his eyes (I think)
we liked the most.
His hands...
he could probably do a lot of things with his hands.

It was good he came
to fix the air conditioner.
It's a lot cooler in here now.

■ EMPTY BED BLUES
KIRSTEN EMMOTT

Some nights
he comes to bed after I'm asleep

Some nights
I work all night in the OR
or sleep at the hospital
don't come home at all

Some nights
I come home at two or three a.m.
crawl in beside him
he makes room for me and cuddles me
without waking up

Some nights
I get called in again at four
he never knows I was there

■ TRYING TO TURN A BAD THING INTO GOOD
SUE DORO

3:20 p.m.

a worse kind of sad
is the second-shift mom
leaving for work
in the afternoon
through no choice
of her own

just in time
to wave at her kids
getting off the school bus
coming home

    3:25 p.m.

    the man in the life
    of the second-shift woman
    washes cast iron
    from his face and hands
    changes clothes
    and starts on his way
    home from work
    knowing she's already gone

    back and forth they travel
    using every minute
    of the earth's rotation
    her eyes are open

his are shut
she's running a machine
he's figuring out
another kid emergency
before he goes to bed
making decisions
in his one head
that could easily use two

they write each other notes
tape record messages
and try not to argue
on the telephone
because it's hell to cry alone

8:00 p.m.

monday through friday
she phones every night
on her 8 o'clock break
from the telephone
in the warehouse
that's the most quiet

then for ten minutes
she listens to her children
grow

says goodbye
hangs up

cries more
'til she cries less
and loves
like a lifetime
full of weekends

3:00 a.m.

second-shift lady
upside-down life
comes home to quiet

let the dog out
let the dog in

eat a little something
take a little bath
climb into a warmed-up bed
to snuggle with
her sleepy first-shift man

■ POST MORTEM
Sandy Shreve

Five o'clock traffic tackled
I deliver my body back home
shed its work-worn parts by yours
already deserted at the door

My mind sprawls on the stairs
in a heap by your aching feet
like clothing clumsily abandoned
for hasty passion...except
the few segments we manage
to drag to the couch
collapse as one in a cuddle
designed for nothing but sleep

But our day-long dreamt-of
nap is disrupted
by our castaways, quibbling
like kids on the steps

My brains gripe at your groaning bones,
"What d'you know about being tired,
we've got mental fatigue –
just danced an eight-hour jig
juggling students' and profs' demands."

Your insides scorn my dreary eyes,
"Try patching plywood hour after hour
inhaling toxic dust all day –
then tell us about how 'bored' and 'sore'
you get from behind your desk!"

Slumber forgotten and sofa vacated
we retrieve our moulted components
misdirected frustrations
released for another week

■ **EXT. 282**
PHIL HALL

When you call me at work
you say my name as a question   *Phil?*
then your name as an answer   *Jane*

an upward and a downward lilt   and yet
they both have the sound of sure arrival

beached waves or the breaking
loose of air-pockets from bird-bone

Before our moaning
parent-seeds these breakers
began to journey here to find
they know me as theirs

and my ears have long unfurled
to cup   channel   be worn deeper
soothed by precisely these

Question-shaped cartilage
receiving you like firelight
through the butterfat
of an infant hand

'til inside I am wave-rocked
tatters of gull-carcass elegant
as an orchid at dawn slopping
back/forth in the shallows –

Forgive me for answering
Editorial

■ EARTH CLINGS TO THE ROOTS
PAT ERWIN SALYER

I swore I'd never marry a farmer.
Got tired of hearing every Saturday,
"You big girls get out of bed and
help your Momma. The beans have to
be picked and the tomatoes canned."
Hated worrying about every hailstorm
and dry spell threatening the tobacco
crop and the possibility of a new dress.
Couldn't abide eating the same pig
I'd slopped for months, hog-killing day,
and everything greasy for a week.
I'd marry a city boy, buy my green beans
in a can at the air-conditioned
Kroger store and bring home faceless
pork on a styrofoam tray. Sleep
half-a-day on Saturdays and have
a regular paycheck. . . a better life.
I thought I'd left it all behind, but
as I turn forty, I find that
I want the earth still clinging
to the little new potatoes Momma
gives me, and early Saturday mornings
I shop the Farmer's Market
for fresh green beans.
The paychecks aren't
regular enough when the plant
lays off, and I silently belittle
the worth of my city man
who doesn't know how to stake
the yellow tomatoes I grow
in the flower bed.

■ PERSPECTIVE
LEONA GOM

my mother in the hayrack
pitching the hay up
into the black box of the loft
where my father's pitchfork took it,

tossed it to the back;
a synchronism asserting itself
through the dry slither of hay,
the pivot of her fork, his fork,
the fulcrum of arm and necessity

until my father's voice – never hers –
saying, *time for a rest*,
and why should I still need to know
if it was because he tired first
or if it was not her right to choose?
And tugging up lately in myself,
like fresh forksful of hay,
a third possibility,
that she refused to give in first,
and a fourth,
that he knew this
and stopped for her sake –
unnerving me
with the increasing complexities
of their lives.

■ STOLEN SUNDAY
SUE SILVERMARIE

At each stop of this half-ton truck
I bend to unlock the collection box,
reach in deep as I can,
sweep the letters into my canvas sack
before the wind can snatch them.

This is the day my son turns 13.
I imagine I'm bringing him birthday letters,
I pretend I'm home, throwing a party.
I see him in a ritual circle
receiving honour, marking passage.

At every stop on this collection route
as I slide open the door and pull from my pocket
the keys attached by a chain to my belt,
I wonder what my son is doing
and whether he knows I love him.

This is the year I hardly see him.
The year we moved 3 times,
the year I've held 4 different jobs,
the year I never met his teachers.
This is the year I'm losing him.

Each time I empty the sack
into the hamper in the back of my truck,
a mother's wishes pour out of my heart
with pictures of birthdays past
when we were poor but I was home.

Back at the unloading dock downtown
the rush of trucks manoeuvre,
each employee in the noisy confusion
eager to return to the family
from whom the Sunday was stolen.

This is the day my boy was born
and I feel as empty as the truck I drive
back to the station, where my car is parked.
I'm afraid I'll be tired and cross.
Is this a year of gain? Or loss...

■ TIME AND A HALF
TODD JAILER

Overtime is a delicacy gobbled
by family men who wipe their mouths
and say Baby needs new shoes.
Whether it's a three hour truck trip
to the mechanics and back, or an hour
plowing the parking lot, Baby
needs new shoes. Some drunk demolishes
a pole and we rise to a 3 AM
call-out muttering new shoes baby
new shoes. After 23 hours repairing
ice storm damage, the lineman
falls into bed and dreams
of watching his children grow
out of their shoes.

■ AS IN THE BEGINNING
MARY DI MICHELE

A man has two hands and when one
gets caught on the belt and his fingers
are amputated and then patched
he cannot work. His hands are insured
however so he gets some money
for the work his hands have done before.
If he loses a finger he gets a flat sum
of $250 for each digit &/or $100 for a joint
missing for the rest of his stay on earth,
like an empty stool at a beggar's banquet.

When the hands are my father's hands
it makes me cry although my pen must keep scratching
its head across the page of another night.
To you my father is a stranger
and perhaps you think the insurance paid is enough.

Give me my father's hands when they are not broken and
    swollen,
give me my father's hands, young again,
and holding the hands of my mother,
give me my father's hands still brown and uncalloused,
beautiful hands that broke bread for us at the table,
hands as smooth as marble and naked as the morning,
give me hands without a number tattooed at the wrist,
without the copper sweat of clinging change,
give me my father's hands as they were in the beginning,
whole,
open,
warm,
and without fear.

■ MY YOUNG BROTHER DON
HOWARD WHITE

The way my young brother Don
flips up a paper
is significant to me.
He's sitting in the good chair

by the stove, legs crossed
with one big boot toward our faces
and he takes the paper
on each side, firm,
and goes "crack"
straightens it and reads,
ignoring our conversation.
He used to be so gentle,
he was the baby,
but he has just come back
from working in the camps.
His voice is growly and loud
as he calls for more tea, he swears
in front of his mother and he
twists the wheel of his
compliant Ford between rough hands.
But still, it is home
he has come to.
It is his father
he rides around all day with
showing these new improvements to
and the first night he is left alone
in the big house
it is my door he comes to,
smiling awkwardly,
    without much
    to say.

■ YOUNGEST IN CANADA
Andrew Wreggitt

Brent, fifteen years old
stands in the door of his parents' house
"I'm goin loggin in a month
Drove a cat last summer, youngest in Canada"
Each word is a challenge thrown at my feet
All down the block
his stereo shakes ravens out of trees
The song says "I don't like you, I don't
like you . . ."
his arms crossed in a knot
against his chest

He startles me with his sureness, his stern face,
the tough frame he has built for his life
His faith is a sleek car
paid for in one summer,
this rumble of drums and guitars,
a coat he wears against the world

Behind him in the harbour
freighters gather up his labour
quotas of wood
What they give back,
new tires, stereos,
"I don't like you, I don't like you..."
An inventory of years on the vibrating machines,
what they give back to anyone

I go home and the music drives on
the way Brent's days will crash
one after another down the slopes of these mountains,
his anger growing for years until it is too big
for music, fast cars,
until the faith is broken

Tonight, he is the youngest in Canada,
his challenge batters the neighbourhood
We who have lived longer in the world
close our windows, the simple beliefs gone out of us,
our anger an older, harder song

WHEN THEY PUSH THE BUTTONS TO RISE
Managerial

■ MY JOB
MICHAEL B. TURNER

I'm paid to watch and work.
I'm the charge-hand.
I'm union and the foreman's my boss.
If you're having problems
I'll let you know.
So don't go running to the foreman.
I'm your boss and I'll do that.

■ TRAITOR
JIM McLEAN

I put my tools away
take a final look around
the rip track silent
in falling snow

but when I turn
to lock the tool box
the tommy bar has climbed back out

Twenty-five years together it says
the words hard as steel
and you'd leave without even saying good-bye

I wanted to, but—

That's longer than most marriages last!
Just goes to show
you never really know someone

Too good for us now the sledge grunts

Listen I say *be reasonable!*
I can't take you with me

We were good enough for him
when he had to earn a living
buy a home, raise a family the bar says
speaking as if I were already gone

How many thousand sill steps
did we straighten for him?
How many grab irons? How many boxes jacked?

Just remember, office boy the sledge booms
when you're sitting there in your 3-piece suit
your feet up on the desk
we won't be there to help you
And there'll be no union
for you to run to when you screw up!

chisels and hammers shout
chains rattle over the edge of the box
wrenches fling themselves at my shins

I stuff them back in the box
slam the lid and lock it

they hammer against the lid, howling
as I walk away

later, I clean out my locker
carry a pair of torn overshoes
and a greasy parka
to the garbage barrel

but I can't do it

and I tell them   *shut up*
hide them
in the trunk of my car

 ■ **HOW CLAYTON GOT TO BE FOREMAN**
Bruce Severy

When Karl the brakeman got squashed between
Two flatcars they called the
Doctor out there rather than to move Karl,
The doctor said the second they
Pulled the cars apart that
Karl would die from shock, if not
He had a few hours, Karl said call

A lawyer, call my family and Pastor Kraft,
Karl was only there from the waist
Up, the doc gave him a shot, made
Him talk real slow but Karl knew the score,
He made his will, he said his prayers, he
Kissed his wife and kids, it was
Time, but the wife
Started in crying and none of the
Guys would pull the cars apart, not even
After the foreman ordered them to, the
Wife said wrap a sheet around Karl's
Lower half, don't move the train, please,
He needs to have his supper first, oh
Please don't do it yet, and Karl
Said I'm a goner, go ahead, but
Nobody moved, then the foreman said
The guy who pulls them cars apart can
Have my job.

■ THIS IS MY NEW JOB
CHIP GOODRICH

This is my new job:
supervising a crew of common criminals
sentenced to "Community Service" in lieu of jail.
We're doing the shit-work
the County Parks Department full-timers
would never get to. Today
hoeing grass out of gravel
around the creosoted stumps planted
along the roadway to keep assholes
from driving across the lawns.

It's boring of course, as befits
punishment, but my cohorts agree
it's better than sitting in a cell.
In fact it's a privilege:
they even had to sign a sheet
of incredibly petty rules (I wrote them)
that begins: "This crew is a privilege…"

No smoking except on breaks.
No radios.
No leaving the work site.
No verbal or physical abuse of the supervisor.

We eat our sack lunches under the picnic shelter,
out of the drizzle for ½ an hour,
talking about nuclear war
and the new stiff penalties
for driving under the influence.
I talk tough, down on the system,
feeling in touch with my criminal element.
They know the difference is I'm getting paid.

But we do a good job. Hey,
might as well put your head down
and make the best of a bad situation.
Kelly rakes up the last batch of weeds.
Gary sweeps off the asphalt.
And Daryl, who's hardly said a word all day, says
"It looks better."

■ THE ADMINISTRATOR'S OFFICE
Jean Flanagan

"A single plug
maintains the heater, radio,
overhead lamp, and computer terminal,"
she says, as she grips a blue china cup.
She points to three stacks,
"Today, tomorrow, and someday."

Tomorrow gets higher
but she never asks for help.
Today we throw time cards
and letters, and invoices
on her desk.

Whenever she gets up to leave,
a webbed metal rest
beside the computer terminal
whacks her back into her seat.

The man in the office next door
told us the one who use to
work in her space went mad
before the terminal.

Each day she buries someday's
in coloured manila folders,
row after row
a flower bed of paper.

We hear her mutter to herself
watch her burn away
slowly and under the surface.

■ COMMITTEE THEORY
RICHARD GROSSMAN

In a large Organization decisions
are rarefied stratified one feels
that nobody ever really makes them:

decisions are formed.

At Gelco you make a decision
you take your life in your hands meaning
a propos of the executive meeting
we sit around discussing

business matters

and make up our minds very carefully
in conformity
with what other members of this committee

are willing for us to say.

■ THE CORNER OFFICE
RICHARD GROSSMAN

To place him in the corner office was an act of vengeance
because he didn't belong there. Trying his entire life
to adjust to a set of immovable circumstances,

he sold a lot of leases but could never sell himself.
There was something he couldn't project because he couldn't
    demonstrate
he had talent. A gaping hole

he tried to fill with little infidelities
and although he was nice he was confused enough
to hurt some people. We gave him the corner office

and he could sit there and look out two sets of windows
and tally up his stock options and count the time
until the whole thing caught up with him

and he would be forced ineluctably out of the company,
never knowing how he had been handled
nor suspecting how much some people knew.

■ CLIMBING
RICHARD GROSSMAN

They huddle eyeball to eyeball
not sure of their reasons for associating
on boats or why their wives go together shopping
but confident that Control works.

It's quite pleasant to socialize effectively;
if you don't want to belong
you give notice

your friends will simply melt away.
They'll find themselves another plateau a nice place

where familiar people sell themselves
for similar sums of money.

■ BUSINESS TAO
RICHARD GROSSMAN

All revolution is an act
to change the standards that people judge by take

the impeccable business suit
worn by a man of the right race

it is a pass to anywhere where
business makes sense an artificial intelligence
would have a hard time

turning down a proposition from such a suit.
A solid appearance is one of those keys

when you know them all and use them
you can break covenants run
Gelco watch the wind

level honest men outside your one
way windows.

■ SPEAKING IN TONGUES
R.W. SANDFORD

November, 1984
at the outset of negotiations involving a
small Western Canadian bus company

they do not hear each other
they wait for their turn to speak

one gestures loudly
overblown
the importance of brotherhood

the other hones the sharp knife
of fiscal reason

slashes at the smoky air

the other pausing briefly
before his next inflated speech

this dark room
in the basement of Babel

the bus seemed unnaturally large
as from the window on the second floor
he watched it turn
through the dusty parking lot
toward the picketers at the exit

the corner was tight
the nervous driver
had to back up once
to face the exit squarely

as the bus approached the street
picketers knotted together
in the centre of the driveway
moving slowly back and forth
over a distance of maybe two meters

the bus approached the pickets
who began hooting and shouting
words he couldn't catch
from where he watched

a man suddenly dropped his sign
and began pounding on the stout mirror
on the passenger side of the bus
the bus edged forward
parting the other pickets
like the blunt bow of a ship
the bus turned
the man dangling from the mirror
narrowly escaping being dragged
under the bus by the tire
that suddenly appeared huge
from the wheel well

the driver couldn't have seen
how close he came to
killing another man

DAY THREE **APPLICATION**
CLASS TWO
FROM PRISON

R.W. Sandford

he claimed
to the switchboard operator
he wanted to apply
for work during the strike
but the warden
wouldn't forward his application
from the prison
where he was innocently confined
for violations
of the unemployment insurance act

I am reminded of the comment
one warden made
of his prison charges

eighty per cent of them
are innocent

just ask them

we have turned
a rock over
and found its bottom surface
teeming

DAY THREE **TRAINING**
R.W. Sandford

The Official Lines: the union strategy
is to take us out
during the only period
in the year when there is
any business

it is a good strategy

or is it

we are forced to operate

Between the lines: it must be made perfectly clear
to each of you that we will be
training you and operating
under desperate conditions

you are strike breakers

we do not know
and we cannot predict
what they will do to you

may God guide you and protect you
may His mercy be upon you

■ DAY TEN   A RESIGNATION LETTER
R.W. SANDFORD

I   won't forget the good times
I   was happy
I   feel sorry not only for the drivers
sticking it out
but for head office people

I hope they get a new president
and management staff

but while you still work there
could you send me one of those pictures
you took of me and the new bus
and maybe a couple of copies of that book
and maybe a few memories of the Icefield Parkway
and since I can't believe you would be on the
company's side in this issue maybe you could
get this stuff to me
by the end of the week

sincerely

■ GRAIG'S TALK
ERIN MOURÉ

He nearly cried when they phoned him,
he says
After working a year wherever they asked,
finally trained as a waiter & liking it:
he's force-assigned in the pantry all summer
tho he didn't bid,
wanting the big money doubling out spare,
dreaming of Asia

On the Main Street bus, together
by chance,
Graig speaks, & holds me captive –
You ain't a service manager here, says Graig
His hurt wears him like
a coat in the close air
He fights thru words, their heaviness
& denigrates the service, the way of seniority
Incompetent, he says
not hearing
my quiet murmur of the gains, worth more
than the risks of being junior:
Now Graig's on the bus & forget it, suckholes –
he's going down to VIA to quit
& go gyprocing
maybe
& Asia will wait

I'm unhappy too, can't struggle at all
thru his tangled feeling
It's no use saying that *the summer is short*
No use that *next year's better*
To him, I'm the Company, & old witless mother

■ BROADVIEW
ERIN MOURÉ

At night you dream you're there, & when
you're there, you dream you're
dreaming, your train frozen in Broadview,

255

& you in the terminal,
bowed over the CP supervisor
whispering
I've got to get these people off the train
Outside it's 120 below with windchill
cuts you as if you weren't there
in your overcoats & mask
as if the wind, as dense as blood
stopped up the sentences

Climbing up again to the cars, 20 below inside,
the passengers stare you down
as if you froze the pipes yourself
their bodies under blankets, too numb to move
waiting for permission,
a place to go, daylight, a dream of coffee

& you living the dream, on & on
the night never ends
Manager of a westbound train, 10 cars of 13 frozen,
crawling the prairie into Broadview,
white-out, crippled, cold
people huddled in bed, fetal
Saying *human*, saying *alive*
so the heart will remember & beat again
Until the van took them safe to the plywood Legion
& you stayed to talk your throat hoarse to Control
Calm because the dream had come to show you,
to understand & grit your teeth,
to take charge, as it dawned on you, the white blast
all night & day at Broadview
until you stepped on the last bus for Regina
& your crew cheered
The dream let go & you sat down, head bowed, weary
where no cold could win you

■ **THE DEPARTMENT HEAD**
GERALD HILL

brown, he says, wearing black
it would be nice not to have to wear brown

256

in the best of all possible worlds, he always says,
we could wear whatever we liked

we wouldn't have to lie to each other
all employees would be treated fairly

although don't get me wrong
we treat you just the same as the permanent staff

just different that's all:
no performance appraisals

no paycheques before the last banking day
separate pigeon holes

you don't get paid for stat. holidays
and we can't guarantee you a job beyond ten weeks

but otherwise we treat you just the same
same hours same job description

same dress code
same photocopy quotas

you get as many pencils as the next guy
so why bother with the union?

■ MANAGEMENT
GERALD HILL

When they push the buttons to rise
to the 8th floor for coffee
a bracelet is exposed on their wrist
a fragment of cologne and was that
a flash of deep brown shoe?

When they step inside the elevator
their chin angles towards the mirror at the top
(except when students get on and crowd to the back)
and their gaze lowers slightly as if
the space is now impure

When they make it to the top how relieved they are
to sit in their jackets facing each other
in a perfect closed circle singing
their management anthem

> *We are the managers*
> *your job is up to us*
> *you can try to hold your ground*
> *the union can try to fuss*
>
> *but we are the managers*
> *you're at our beck and call*
> *the clearest way to put it is*
> *we've got you by the balls*

                              and they all
shake the tassels on their loafers and make
PR and watch themselves on the monitors

They especially like
the scenes of themselves jolly as if
they're a pack of fools who enjoy
cuts to staff programs service enrollment and space
because their solemn duty of management is complete
when nothing is left but themselves
safe in their mahogany pods

LESS LIKE ANTS
Assessment and Resistance

WORKER CLASSIFICATION: MATERIAL HANDLER
GLEN DOWNIE

We work in the world you and I handling
coal chandeliers razor blades hamburger
whatever they ask us to carry sort shovel
A box of glass eyes or tear gas cartridges
Mud silk marshmallows guns potatoes...
One man handles diamonds   another garbage
Chalk or cheese   we come home stained
skinned   stinking

I have wiped the asses of grown men
You've smashed up old batteries
the splashed acid eats at your jeans
Do we work because we're hungry
for substance   Is it even lonelier
for mathematicians

Pat cuts off a cancerous breast
The day's work has begun   How does it feel
when a severed breast slips off into your hand
Catherine dresses up stillborns in the morgue
so parents can say goodbye
The babies are cold and pale as congealed fat
I ask her   How do you handle a dead baby

This is the way the world works: you are building a house
as I tear it down   We need each other
Hands must be full of something
Who knows how we came to be here
We are groping like the newly blind
for anything familiar
for anything at all

PAPER, SCISSORS, STONE
TOM WAYMAN

An executive's salary for working with paper
beats the wage in a metal shop operating shears
which beats what a gardener earns arranging stone.

261

But the pay for a surgeon's use of scissors
is larger than that of a heavy equipment driver removing
    stone
which in turn beats a secretary's cheque for handling paper.

And, a geologist's hours with stone
nets more than a teacher's with paper
and definitely beats someone's time in a garment factory with
    scissors.

In addition: to manufacture paper,
you need stone to extract metal to fabricate scissors
to cut the product to size.
To make scissors you must have paper to write out the specs
and a whetstone to sharpen the new edges.
Creating gravel, you require the scissor-blades of the crusher
and lots of order forms and invoices at the office.

Thus I believe there is a connection
between things
and not at all like the hierarchy of winners
of a child's game.
When a man starts insisting
he should be paid more than me
because he's more important to the task at hand,
I keep seeing how the whole process collapses
if almost any one of us is missing.
When a woman claims she deserves more money
because she went to school longer,
I remember the taxes I paid to support her education.
Should she benefit twice?
Then there's the guy who demands extra
because he has so much seniority
and understands his work so well
he has ceased to care, does as little as possible,
or refuses to master the latest techniques
the new-hires are required to know.
Even if he's helpful and somehow still curious
after his many years –
again: nobody does the job alone.

Without a machine to precisely measure
how much sweat we each provide
or a contraption hooked up to electrodes in the brain
to record the amount we think,
my getting less than him
and more than her
makes no sense to me.
Surely whatever we do at the job
for our eight hours – as long as it contributes –
has to be worth the same.

And if anyone mentions
this is a nice idea but isn't possible,
consider what we have now:
everybody dissatisfied, continually grumbling and disputing.
No, I'm afraid it's the wage system that doesn't function
except it goes on
and will
until we set to work to stop it

with paper, with scissors, and with stone.

ONTARIO EQUAL PAY RALLY & CELEBRATION
(May 15/86)
GWEN HAUSER

the cake
        is a joke
you want to
            throw in
the organizer's
            face:

the icing
        is like
shaving cream,
            the cake proper
like
    someone's kitchen
sponge:

nobody dances
            to the music
the balloons
            are nuisances
that don't
        get off
            the ground

after all
        who can
celebrate
        for equal pay
for 2%
        of the women's
                work-force?*

we circle the legislature
with black-and-white
                streamers –
the only fitting thing:
                they *aren't*
gaily coloured
            & look like

bureaucrats'
            strands of red tape
                    or typewriter ribbons...

*The Equal Pay Amendments only
cover the public sector – 2% of the
women's workforce, according to the
Toronto Star.

■ **E = MC² (PAY DAY)**
GWEN HAUSER

pay day came
        once every
2 weeks.

you could
        always

tell because
        everyone
brought out
        their microscopes

to examine
        their microscopic
pay-cheques
        with

(sometimes
        the digits
disappeared
        to infinity
& everyone
        was left
contemplating
            the Black Holes
in Einstein's
            universe
            (or whoever it was
        that
            discovered them))

:pay cheques
            were always
the best examples
        of his Theory
of Relativity
            anyways...

you had
        to be
careful
        or you'd lose

your pay-cheque
        because it was
so small:
        the best thing was
to pin it
        inside
your pocket-
        book

■ THE BIG THEFT

Tom Wayman

for Howard White

It's one of those myths
from the workplace, told by somebody who is sure
the story is true. So you believe it, until

you find yourself listening to another version
of the tale. In this case
let's call it The Big Theft. I first heard it
in a truck assembly plant:

before you came, Tom, there was a guy,
Roger Hutchison, worked here:
an oldtimer. The guard caught him
at the gate one afternoon
leaving with an oil pressure gauge in his lunchkit.
Hell, we all take something home
if we can use it—clips or seat cushions—
Roger was just unlucky and got nabbed.
But for some reason they went around to his house
and discovered a nearly-completed truck
in his garage. Over the years, he had boosted
piece by piece almost everything for it.
He'd obviously gotten help moving the larger items
like the frame or the engine
from the parts yard. But he had built
pretty damn close to an entire tractor unit
in his spare time.

                       Then at coffee
on a renovation job:
Donny used to be employed at a brickworks
where a man each day
took a brick home in his lunchbox.
Only one brick. But when the man dropped dead of a heart
    attack
the week before he was due to retire
they found he had stockpiled
a few bricks less than the total he needed
to construct his dream house.

How this myth began isn't hard to grasp.
Even the dullest among us can understand
no amount of money the company pays
really compensates for the time and effort
the job takes out of our lives.
As the slogan says: *the things we give up*
to go to work
are never returned. It's pleasant to imagine
some person someplace turning the tables.

And as with every myth, there's a lesson here.
This teaches we can gain possession
of what we make where we are employed
but not by acting alone.

Plus, it is evident
rent-a-cops aren't posted at the office door at quitting time
to check the executives' briefcases
or certain envelopes addressed to the owners.
If these containers were opened
inside would be revealed
part of the value of the labour we perform each shift
being snuck out past the fence.
What these people remove secretly
isn't material required on this job
so they don't consider their actions stealing.
Yet from our work
a group of men and women get richer than us
without even asking us to vote
on whether we consent to this situation.
And that's
no myth.

■ CLOSURE
Susan Meurer

The business report in the
Globe & Mail hardly
takes up two inches of newsworthiness.
Goodyear Canada Inc.
"Profit for six months ended June
30, 1987, $12.4 million compared

with $7.3 million a year earlier."
But I know who earned every dollar
to make the two inches possible.

I've heard the days that make up
a $5 million working lifetime at a tire plant.
I spent a week with Mike, Alan, Leo, Gary, Fitzroy...

On May 1 they became statistics
in a plant closure ledger.
Not even an ink stain in the company books.
Tire builder, compounder, mold man, bead man:
they created the $5 million.

What am I to think
of a company that reports record profits
when 1200 workers are terminated.
Some severance, early retirement,
six months of benefits, do these equal
a working life?

So I consider: what is $5 million
divided by 1200?
"Share profit $4.80 compared with
$2.81."
I see that the creators of the wealth
lose their jobs to ensure $2 profit increase
for those who never
         moved 40,000 tires a year;
         built 250 radials a shift;
         mixed tonnes of tire compound;
         worked one hour in a tire plant.

■ HEALTH AND SAFETY
Susan Meurer

Just when I think – and others like me
         I'm certain too –
that it's time to mellow, to soften,
         to round my edges a bit,
Another worker dies on the job:
         Falls from a scaffold;

Has been caught in a machine;
Is overcome by toxic fumes;
Suffers a heart attack from stress.
Anger rises in me, anger, not sorrow
And I ask myself again,
as too many times before,
How long.

I attend another union meeting and sit
with retirees and near retirees,
Anything but the picture of health.
I wonder about the brothers and sisters
we don't see,
names and ages listed under "Sick" or "Deaths."
The slow poison of a job is the
worker's only surplus value,
Cell for cell the body gives way, as
Dollar for dollar, profits increase.
I don't know how long I can look on,
research, educate, write,
When it's all a baby finger in the
dike of genocide.
Each time I see a worker with body parts missing –
Fingers, joints, legs, an eye,
My mental calculator ticks off more numbers,
The total reaches new highs.

Some day, a long line of us, bill in hand,
Maybe even on a silver tray,
Will queue up at mahogany row,
Demanding payment.
Visa won't do.
No WCB claim.
And not danger premiums either.
This time the price is a fair one.

■ TO A WORKER NEVER KNOWN
SUSAN MEURER

I never met Dennis Huntley,
Not in the fifty years he lived,
Nor in the Mississauga company

Where he worked.
But we all now know what
Dennis Huntley was worth:
$15,000.
That is the cost of working with acetone,
That is the price of third degree burns,
That is the value of Dennis Huntley's job:
A life.
What is the cost analysis
for Provost Cartage?
>   a few months of executive salary;
>   a trip for three bosses to a conference in Dallas;
>   new broadloom for the corporate offices.
What are the costs we don't calculate:
>   To Dennis Huntley's wife,
>   To his children,
>   To his grandchildren yet unborn,
>   To the kids he coached at hockey,
>   To the neighbours he helped on weekends,
>   To the buddies he saw up north,
To all of us who are the poorer
For losing another among us.

The day the $15,000 fine was announced,
A world was concerned with saving
>   Three grey whales.
As millions worried, no effort too great,
As millions were spent on a rescue operation,
Dennis Huntley was given a price.
And passed unnoticed on page 36.

■ GRIEVANCE PROCEDURE
SANDY SHREVE

I am listening to
a woman worried –
the harassment's there
though often so subtle
it evades articulation.

Not that she wants to grieve
this incident, or that
in union terms

(the concept of defiance
such a threat)

And yet she grieves –
trying hard not to cry, she
apologizes as I
offer tissues:

feeble things, only good
for absorption.

The office trashcan, congested
with such as these,
an archive of pain
collected and dumped
each day

■ THE GRIEVANCE
RHONA McADAM

I have grieved to the union
and the whole of the workplace
grieves with me. It is a sad
sad day, and the grief of the workers
spills from their fingers
to weep green tears
on the glass pages
of their computer screens.

I have grieved to the union
and the bosses are grim
and their mouths are pencil lines
of despair. There is misery
in the panelled reaches
of the building; and even
in the upholstered chairs there is
a mounding sadness

and steepled fingers probing the silence
for comfort.

I have grieved to the union
and in the cafeteria they shake their heads
with such sadness their hair
droops from their hair nets. And even
the dishes are unhappy, and spring holes
so their contents wash the table tops
with dismay; and there is a wailing
at coffee break that finds its way
to the glass ceiling, where the sky
lowers its crepe veil.

I have grieved to the union,
I have painted myself with the brush
of sorrow; I have cast myself in a wilderness
of despair, and from this exile
I will have the last laugh.

■ SORRY I'M LATE
PAM TRANFIELD

but
I woke up with my period and found
my box of tampons had turned to dandelions,
gone to seed just like on the TV ads.

I left for work, early, in my new ruby slippers
and an awful wind took me from the bus stop
carried me all the way to K-Mart
into the arms of a scientologist
buying oil in the hardware section.
He helped me
find myself, my shoes.

In the elevator
a supervisor smelled my briefcase
told me
tuna sandwiches have been banned
in the secretarial pool.

(I snacked between the 8th and 11th floors
and had to wash my face).

Honestly, I woke up in time but
my Harley-Davidson is missing a cylinder
I had to move Mozart from the shower
I swear the calendar read 1958
the cat knocked over the moon
        I slept in.

■ POLITICS OF VIEW
STEPHEN LEWANDOWSKI

In front of our factory
the company's just dug
a huge pit.
Once the money is spent
to dig the hole,
water can't be speeded,
stopped or slowed.
It leaks in & falls from the sky.
It collects in a reflection
holding a 2nd complete factory.
The company is proud
of its cost-effectiveness:
a 2nd factory at a pond's cost.

We who work the night shift
at machines which extrude
plastic meat trays
have no windows. We won't
be distracted by the view.

But we do get to see the pond,
as we roar out the gate
in the morning,
through chain-link fence.

■ HAS ANYONE SEEN THE WORKING CLASS?
HOWARD WHITE

A young American woman with a PhD has written me
saying she wants to devote her life to the working class
and can't decide if it should be in some third-world country
or Canada. I haven't been able to reply for over a year
although I feel an uncertain responsibility
to speak up for our bunch

A friend I owe much to has put her up to this
after reading some things I wrote about driving cat
and I struggle to be worthy
of their confidence: *the working class*
the *Canadian* working class – oh thou elusive wraith,
long have I avoided this moment of truth

I think of my brother who still gets dirty for money
– but pulls down more in a year than the local doctor

I think of the Communist Party and its confident talk
of a Canadian proletariat – but then at election time
polling fewer votes than the Rhinoceros Party

I think of the time that student marxist group at UBC
got carried away with its own talk
and marched down to free the embattled workers at Canron
and the Canron bosses had to call the riot squad in
to stop the men from leaving their work
to pound the piss out of these damnfool students

I think of all those loggers I grew up with
how they would turn away from any attempt
to class them together, especially
as any sort of underprivileged species
– the funny look that would pass between them
when some hapless tourist came to camp
and made the mistake of saying "you fellows..."
in that special class self-conscious way...

I think of how those young guys wanted so much to be rich,
to go to Hawaii and drive a new Cadillac

instead of a ten-year-old one
as long as this wouldn't turn them into shits

I think of how some did just that
and liked it fine
although they didn't do so good

at not becoming shits

I think of how the gillnet fishermen
used to mock their ever-so-serious union rep
and how they didn't care to hear
that what they thought was a proud career
was just some smarter men making monkeys of them
I think of how the one word I never heard
in the working class town where I grew up
was the word working class

The more I think about it the more the Canadian working
    class
takes on the shape of some impossible fiction

until this one Saturday in January Sticks Andersen
a salt-soaked old troller who's been around forever
is sitting in my kitchen bitching about the price of
    live-landed lingcod

and another neighbour, a nice-enough guy from the city
who has never worked with his hands and has a bigger house
for weekends than we do for all year round
comes tapping at the door to see if we can help him
start this little bitty powersaw he got for Christmas.
He's got the operator's manual memorized
but cranks it like a baby –
one good snap is all it takes
and he's tickled as hell – "I was afraid I had a lemon," he says

We can see he'll never get the load of firewood
he wants for his new French parlour heater
he'll saw both feet off first
but Sticks doesn't want to make him feel bad
so he says, "By God, I could use some wood..."

and we lead the guy back in the bush with our own battered
    Stihls

"What size wood does that there new boiler of yours take?"
Sticks asks and we rip through a bunch of nice downed fir
as our friend frets and fusses with this saw
measuring off each cut with a steel tape –

"We mustn't mix up our pieces," he cautions us with
    irritation
tugging his few hard-clawed chunks away from the growing
    pile

"Well, you know, this is comin pretty easy here," Sticks says,
"Why don't you just pull your bus up here and we'll throw on
    a load."
"But most of this is *yours*..." the guy stammers,
realizing for the first time we've cut every piece to his size,
"I couldn't let you...you must take some for yourselves..."
"Ah, me'n Speedy here can get wood any time," Sticks
    replies.
"This is worth money..." the other mumbles,
digging out keys to his new Cherokee Chief and breaking into
    a trot

leaving Sticks and I standing there confronted
once again
by all the difference that is class

■ THE UNOFFICIAL REPORT
DALE HALL

The federal gov't held a
conference where I worked
Tables set in silver, chandeliers
and prosperity
The session was on women
and work
I watched them – those concerned
delegates as they ambled in
They wore their best attire
shaking hands & smiling with security

As the older women dressed appropriately as
maids served their dinner
scraped the plates
the Portuguese women in the kitchen
gossiped about how lovely everyone
looked
I wonder what the delegation on
working women would have done
had we all marched in &
thrown our trays to the floor
showed them our swollen feet
and our disfigured spines
When the dishes were all cleared away
they settled back to liqueurs & coffee
to discuss the future of working women
While we scraped 90 cents in change out of
the bottoms of our purses to catch the
subway home

I wonder why no one asked me how
I felt about working women!

AT THE GRAND OPENING (OF THE NORTHEAST COAL PROJECT)
Brett Enemark

for Wally MacKay and Mike Zelt
(who were there too)

I envy you
said the minister for economic development to a crowd
of miners and construction workers

I envy you
said the former used-car salesman to a crowd mixed with
business executives, politicians, reporters and a film crew

I envy you
he said, having just stepped from a helicopter to a
stage shared with the premier in front of the new town hall

I envy you
he said, at a ceremony costing the public some one
hundred and fifty thousand dollars

I envy your 8 by 10 rooms in long white trailers
     (particle board, two inch walls, broken mirrors)

I envy you
moving your family from one company town to another

I envy your mortgage
        in a town that tomorrow may disappear

I envy your old mortgage
        on a house you can't sell
        in a town that no longer exists

I envy you, shot dead for interfering in a wife-beating
        in the next room

I envy you
   driving sixty miles over a winding dirt road
               to get drunk in Chetwynd

I envy you
   heading back to camp so pissed you see the truth
                  & turn around

I envy you
         crushed to death between two airtracks

I envy you
     lying so quietly under your packer (overturned)
        or resting forever beneath a mudslide

I envy you
     driving a rock wagon over a mountain
        falling backwards into a waste dump

I envy you, drugged by gasses, losing consciousness
   sinking, your face in hot asphalt body rising
       up a conveyer belt cooked at 200 degrees
         found in the back of a truck

I envy you
> scabbing for four bucks an hour
>> living in a cardboard box

I envy you
> paving your walls and ceilings
>> with air-brushed nudes

I envy you
> on your birthday waking up in bed
>> with a blow-up doll

I envy you
> having lost all purpose
>> but your own survival

I envy you
> crawling down the hall in a trail of vomit
>> searching for your glasses

I envy you
> fishing in a freshly poisoned river

■ IN THE BRIEF INTERVALS BETWEEN THEIR STRUGGLES OUR PEOPLE DREAM
ERIN MOURÉ

> *"#4, you're on the Main..."*
> ■ CN brakeman to engineman

In the 4th setting of dinner, the trees
brush past them, waiters & stewards
memorize the orders, dreaming the last Super-
Continental,
the tale-end of a job after
all those promises

Later, they clean
beneath tables, the diner hurtles into night
where the tracks are laid for it,
its subsidy,
its workers are struggling but still have dreams:

Of taking over, the day after cutback;
if all the rail unions
could stand together
& run the Super thru
against all orders, cut in the cars
in Vancouver terminal, change the brake-shoes;
the waiters dream of
carmen checking the A/C relays,
ticket agents selling tickets without ReserVIA,
on-board personnel reporting
in uniform
tho they're laid off & finished,
the enginemen coming to drive,
dispatcher & crew routing the Super
out to the mainline,
full of passengers,
its cars shimmer & groan on the switches,
its diner in full service, porters
spreading white sheets over the berths,
smiling, the passenger assistant coming at each meal
with reservations,
Pepin in an uproar as the Super looms closer to Ottawa,
Roberts eating his quotes in the Globe & Mail,
the Super not a runaway but a train
unrescinded,
crossing the country in 4 days on schedule,
manned by rail workers
deaf to government intervention,
who are their train & run it surely,
who become their dreams

■ THE TRUCKDRIVER
HOWARD WHITE

It would be easy to talk about all the terrible accidents
we used to get into, but in all honesty I don't know how
    much worse it was
you'd see a man get killed once in a while just like you do now
I don't think anybody's been keeping score
God knows it shoulda been worse,
    when you compare what we did
sitting out in the open on a board seat

couple three-thousand-foot logs jiggling around
        behind your head
no bulkhead for protection wheel straining
        like a mad pig in your hands
trying to stay on those plank trestles with hard rubber tires
oh, a bit of mud or frost on those planks and it didn't matter
if you had brakes or not, looking down through a hundred feet
It was a different life, and it wasn't just the danger or the
        work
— it's hard to talk about it to anyone who wasn't there.
These big new Pacifics and Kenworths we have now,
        I don't know how
you could ever get into trouble, but they do.
When I first went hauling logs in the thirties
        we had three-ton Fords
old Bill Schnare had seized off farmers around the Fraser
        Valley
most of them had no doors or windows
        and we would bring single logs
with more scale in them than whole loads they get today
rattling and banging our way down Vedder Mountain,
        but nobody got hurt
on that job. We had those haywire old trucks working so good
you couldn't imagine it being done any better.
You got so you could hear the truck.
You'd had the goddamn thing apart
        so many times you were aware
of every goddamn bearing and how it was turning.
You'd see a new grease spot on the ground in the morning
and think, 'that Christly packing's come out again'
and if you didn't strip it down right there
        at least you'd make sure
it didn't run dry of oil that day. If the brakes started to go
you'd sense the slight change in the pedal, or you'd have
        caught
the wet spot on the wheel and be looking for it.
You got to where nothing was an accident; it's always
you missed something or let something go.
        You weren't on the job.
And if you did get in a jam you knew how to get out of it.
Say you lose your brakes – the cooling water plugs up
        and the brakes burn up.

A driver who isn't with it doesn't know what's happening until
he's freewheeling down the mountain and there's nothing to do
but jump and knock his brains out on a stump.
The seasoned driver would have spotted the steam
        starting to thin out
five, ten minutes earlier and had time to do something.
The green guy, even if he did catch that,
        would dynamite right there
and push his hot brakedrums all out of shape,
        or else go for the ditch
and end up putting the load through the cab and getting
        smeared.
The other guy starts looking for the right spot to go off
where the trailer will hang up before the truck
and within an hour he's back on the road hauling logs.

Even a little thing like a mud puddle. You'll see the one guy
go half off the road to miss a
        little puddle the size of a dinner plate
then your cowboy comes ploughing straight through it,
the cold splash breaks the red-hot drums, the truck runs away
and they tell his widow, 'oh, the brakes failed.'
Today of course, with the miracle alloys they have, you never
have to think about anything like that. These young fellows
wouldn't live to see lunchtime on one of our old jobs,
        but try to tell them.
It's not that they're made out of such inferior stuff it's just
that in today's world the worker is given so much less to do.
This is the real change I've seen:
        it used to be the tools we had
were so minimal the only way you could survive was
by putting a hell of a lot of yourself into the job.
Jobs took years to learn, but once you'd done it
you could write your own ticket.
It was possible to achieve a sort of greatness in that work.
Now the genius has all been put into the machines
and all that's required of the worker is a kind of dumb
        obedience.
There's been a loss of scale, of human scale
but if you try to talk about it
they just look at you like you were crazy.

O THE LIONS OF FIRE
WAIT IN THE CRAWLING SHADOWS OF YOUR WORLD
AND THEIR TERRIBLE EYES ARE WATCHING YOU

■ *Kenneth Patchen*

ROGER TAUS

On Monday
I'm called into the office
and offered the choice
of quitting now or getting
fired later.
The steelyard has become a zoo
with electrified bars.
Without organized resistance
these fascists
can crumple us up like scrap paper
at will.

The last shots come
Thursday afternoon.
I'm cornered like a rat
by the boss
in warehouse three.
He is robbing me
of my living
just as if he had a gun.
The new steward
sits on his forklift like a fat old judge
and says nothing
in my defence.

I have talked unity,
talked back, built nothing.
After a year and a half
in this place
I return to the car
one last time.
I get in and start driving
only to fall apart
sobbing in my wife's arms
for several whole minutes
by the side of the road.

■ BLUE COLLAR GOODBYES
Sue Doro

blue collar goodbyes are a jumpstart
on a frozen battery midnight parking lot
peering out of second shift propped open coffee eyes
wide as inch and a quarter sockets
from a tool box back at the radial drill machine
in Allis Chalmers tractor shop
where the only Black man on the housing line
teams up with the only female in maintenance repair
to move those tractors out the door

now Bill Dunlap's powerful hands fasten jumper cables
to plus and minus inside car hoods exposed to Winter in
        Wisconsin
my '71 Ford and Bill's bran' new step-up van's competent
        motor
vibrating powdered snow like sifted cake flour
off a gleaming waxed finish revealing
Bill's stencil painted signature design
DADDY HIGH POCKETS and his wife Bernice,
LADY LOW POCKETS in the cold moon glow blue
        brightness

as my engine finally turns over
warming up goodbyes satisfying
as Bill and Bernice's faces across their kitchen table
heavy with platters of deep Southern fried catfish
and hot corn bread put out for company
my home partner Larry and I over for Saturday night

and Bill waits inside his van to be sure
I'm not stuck in ice ruts
then Bill's gone, I'm gone, Allis Chambers gone
fifteen years and a plant closure later

blue collar goodbyes become letters and phone calls
from back home Bill and Bernice
and Milwaukee Road buddies Earl, Don and Verona
veterans of yet another plant closing down, another buy-out
by a hungrier corporation

another selling out up the hill
with nothing but our lunch buckets
more forced layoffs, a few paid severances,
don't know how many transfers to Chicago or Minneapolis
where the Soo Line promised jobs then
four years later about to go belly up too,
it offers those same people a chance to buy their own failing
    railroad
in a town they never wanted to live in

blue collar goodbyes report Wisconsin to California
on lined school notebook paper stark and strong
THERE'S BACK PAY COMING...YOU BETTER CALL
and phoning find the Soo Line would've kept my blood
    earned money
if I had not been told, if I had not known

but corporate minds will never know the hearts of survivors
of shutdowns and 40 below zero wind chills
work friends like family separated by job change and cross
    country miles
people who hold dear and remember lunch buckets
Saturday catfish and goin' home car rides that never say never
'cause we'll see you sometime
goodbyes like sparks of electricity
through jumper cables in a midnight parking lot

■ MARGARET'S PARTY
JONI MILLER

today everyone quits working
ten minutes early
and scuttles down
to the lunchroom.

margaret is retiring
25 years of service
"put it this way" graham says
"when margaret was a girl
i was still a kid
when margaret was a woman
i was still a boy"

we took up a collection
and the company matched it
luggage – we bought her luggage
everyone signed the card.

we all jam into the smoky lunchroom –
(not designed to hold all of us at once)
simon presents the gift
because he's the boss
he makes a joke   but nobody gets it

25 years
margaret fumbles with the wrapping
"no need to save the paper – today"
simon says
he is being generous.

25 years
faces she's known
in coffee breaks and lunch breaks
and across the noisy shop
say "make a speech"

margaret's never made a speech
and she doesn't like
everyone staring at her
"thanks" she says

25 years of service.
everyone punches out at 5:30
like usual.

■ ICON IN RYE
BRUCE HUNTER

his retirement party
they're staging it like a crucifixion
at sixty-three retirement forced
with wine and cheese for the guy
who always drank rye out back
with the boys from shipping
the boss is there standing guard

over the old man full of bile and cancer
who calls me aside:
son of a bitch
that's not wine
but blood he's drinking
my blood

the ladies from the kitchen
there among his friends
few despite the show of president
vice presidents and various secretaries
finally it's time
they roll in the cake
on the cart full of gifts
among them the obligatory watch

later he tells the guys from shipping
a watch?
me, i got no use for time
they nod and under the table
top the wine glasses with rye

■ RETAKE THE CITY
Robert Carson

Why do these dreams recur –
The tender, the brutal –
Never allowing a separation
to savour or scorn just one.

Dreams of light,
sleight of hand,
Elongation of a raindrop
freefalling
reaching out to splatter
on cement and steel.

The last heavy-veined leaf
from all the branches of thought –
A work partner pummelled to eternity
head first in a glorious swandive.

Slipping on a containership,
the steel and cement closing down...

Dull thud we all pretended
not to hear.

A clerk, clipboard in hand,
squashed against a 20 ton container
scattered over a retaining wall.
Don't slip on his liver.

Flowing days
of all our futures.
We set to work
Knowing the water, fog, light,
cement and salt.

These are dreams
and these are realities
into which we all
have fallen
and daily return
suspended like bridges
over the final bay of the world.

Bells toll,
Crossing Dolores Park,
Portsmouth Square, Washington Square.
Whirling tones –
Bells, Colours –
Tones of work partners
Spiralling through space.

City of generations
Who all have fallen
in dreams' gentle violence.
The leaf separated from the tree
falling over the edge of memory.

Bells for forgotten men.
Wanderers, Workers, Poets.
Returning home

The tones of dusk in watercolour.
The sun mixing with the sea

Bells that toll for survival:
Everyday you must remake,
Everyday you must reshape,
Everyday you must retake
The city.

■ IT'S ALL OUR FAULT
AL GRIERSON

it's all our fault –
we killed the redwoods
and now we're ready to take the blame
and pay the money that we get paid
to see them protected in national parks
that we don't own.

we're the people who fished out the oceans
so our kids could eat oatmeal
and day old bread
and now we're waiting out the moratorium
on the catching of roe herring,
waiting also for the first unemployment cheque
and the kids are eating oatmeal
without sugar but we're not complaining –
it's all our fault.

we're the people who followed the boom
and brought the oil out of the ground
to fuel the cars that others of us made
so they could eat
and we're the people who built the roads
we use to get to places
where we build more cars, more roads
and better mousetraps
and now that we have to wear gasmasks
and listen to smog alerts, we're sorry –

it's all our fault.

we're the people who are ruining the economy
with our outrageous wage demands:
father forgive us, for we understand not
the ways of inflation.

we're the people who destroyed
the institution of marriage and the sanctity
of the nuclear family
by not resisting the sexual advances
of our bosses –
it's all our fault; we should have had
more personal integrity.

we killed the whales, the seals,
the buffalo and each other,
we poisoned the air, polluted the water,
and made this a planet
fit only for insects.

we did it for wages;
it's all our fault –
we did it because we didn't know
there was anyone else to go to work for.

■ **THE WAY I FIGURE IT**
  ANTLER

The way I figure it
No one should be a slave.
Everyone should be free.
When I think of my own life
            I think Wow,
Already I've worked over five years
            in factories!
For working that long I deserve
            the rest of my life
            to be a paid vacation.
Then I start thinking of my mother
            and brother and sister
            and friends
Chained to jobs they have to put up with,
Yet my father being dead is free from all that,

But when I think how he only got
        a three-week vacation every year,
Or how the 12-hour day 6-day workweek for pittance
        was once taken for granted,
When people got a one-week vacation
        in their 20s or 30s
Or a two-week vacation
        in their 40s or 50s...
I've got to make up for them by golly!
Why, every day a person works in a factory
I figure that gives them a year's vacation,
So boy oh boy, I gotta lotta vacations
        to live in a single life!
Maybe I'll give a few out to you
        my friends and readers.
Maybe if we all realize we should be
        all making up for the wasted lives
(So many now in the history of humans
        each of us would have to live a million lives
        to make up for all their lost vacations)
We can get back in touch with the time
        we were less like ants
And more like eagles soaring
        over the wilderness realms of the earth.

WRITTEN AFTER LEARNING SLAVES IN ANCIENT GREECE AND ROME HAD 115 HOLIDAYS A YEAR
Antler

Instead of creating better murder weapons
        to "protect" ourselves,
Better create loving boys and girls
        who become loving women and men.
Instead of a higher standard of living
        why not a higher standard of loving?
Why not a higher standard
        of getting high?
No more brainwashed robotzombies!
No more socialization lobotomies!

Thoreau could live a whole year
              on money from working 6 weeks.
We canned ourselves in concentrationcamps
              called cities
And in buildings and rooms where we work.
We have become hermetically sealed containers.
The can of today is the wilderness that was.
The can-to-be is the wilderness that is.

As Oscar Wilde said: "Work is the curse
              of the drinking man."
As Stan Jones said: "It's not what the machine makes,
              but what the machine makes you."
As Virgil said: *Deus nobis haec otia fecit*:
              "A god has granted us this idleness."
As Lessing said: "Let us be lazy in everything
              except in loving and drinking,
              except in being lazy."

Should cans stop being made?
Should all factories immediately close down?
What solution do you provide? If everyone's a poet
              and no one works, how do we survive?
The way St. Theresa survived on Light?
Love becomes a full-time job?
But where do we get the money
              to pay people not to work?

Slaves in Ancient Greece and Rome
                            had 115 holidays a year!
Hey, wait a minute, that makes us
                    more slaves than them!

■ ZERO-HOUR DAY ZERO-DAY WORKWEEK
ANTLER

Are the executives of oil steel aluminum plastic
              military industrial capitalism
To be looked up to as Great Men and Women to be held
              as fitting examples of enlightened human beings?
Or are they miserable failures of greed who betray the Earth
              and the promise of America?

Is who invented napalm to be honoured?
Is who invented nervegas to be honoured?
Slavery did not end. Almost everyone enslaved
        to earthdeath accomplice jobs.
A new Emancipation Proclamation is needed.
Liberation from an 8-hour day 5-day workweek
        to a 5-hour day 1-day workweek
        getting paid the same amount.
Or how about a 12-hour day 7-day playweek?
Or maybe keep only the least harmful factories
        and everyone has to factory once for year,
        the rest of their life free to learn and create,
        travel to wilds and other lands, like Huxley's *Island*?

We think working 8 hours a day
        a great advance over the time
        when workers, even children,
        worked 14 hours a day
        for lousy wages and conditions.
It *is* better, but 8 hours a day
        is still too long!
Our lives should be free, a continual vacation.
Anyone who had to work all their life
        and had a two-week vacation every year
        has been robbed.
Anyone who had to work six months a year
        and had a six-month vacation
        has been robbed.
Anyone who had to work one day a year
        and had a 364-day vacation
        has been robbed.
Only Total Vacation will do.

Expand Wilderness, Reduce Population, Reduce Production!
Anyone who says it can't be done is performing what I call
        "The Ghost Dance In Reverse."
We can shape the Image of Man we desire!
We can shape the Image of Boy we desire!
We can shape the Image of Girls and Women and America
        and World Peace and Wilderness VisionQuest Enlightenment
        we desire!

A 12-hour day 6-day workweek
        becomes a 10-hour day 6-day workweek
        becomes an 8-hour day 5-day workweek
        becomes a 6-hour day 4-day workweek
        becomes a 4-hour day 2-day workweek
        becomes a 1-hour day 1-day workweek
        becomes a 0-hour day 0-day workweek!

People should be paid not to work!
People should be paid to play!
People should lie in hammocks
        and sip lemonade all day!
Most people are too busy working or resting from work
        to work on their own mindgrowth poet-ential.
"But," my mother asks, "what about workers who *like*
        their jobs – happy they receive so much money
        to buy all the amazing things factories make
        not to mention the benefits they get
        for medical protection and old age?"
It's not religion that's the opium of the people, but *work*,
Work is the opium of the people. O Workers of the World,
        stop working!
Think of the whales, more intelligent than Einstein or Bach,
        who never have to work a fucking second
        of their incredible life!

■ AND YOU KNOW IT
Sadhu Binning

no answer
to my good morning
she stares at the bag
and always with a deep sigh:
'is that whole thing for us?'
her heavy makeup
fails miserably
to hide her weariness
her tired and suppressed voice
speaks loudly
of open exploitation
of a boss/servant relation

of course she can never dare
to express things this way
all workers in the office
are part of a 'big happy family'

and then enters
the boss
with big round stomach
first in sight
(another proof the earth is round)
in a commanding voice
he demands
'is that all you have for us?'
propelling words
his rotten breath
almost touching my eyebrows

he further interrogates
'hey what is it i hear
you guys
going on strike again?'
doesn't wait for my answer
'you sure are crazy
never understand
soon as you get a raise
the prices will just fly up
(throws his arms upward in the air,
on the way down a finger from his
hand starts shaking while staring
straight into my eyes)
you'll never catch up
and you know it'

it makes me feel
like a prisoner
when told by the guard
'don't try to run
my dogs will catch you
and rip you apart
and you know it'

■ RHETORIC
DALE ZIEROTH

Ours is not the only strike
in the news: one man
has been dragged by a truck
through the picket line;
outside movie theatres
trade unionists have lined up
to jostle those who need
their entertainment fix.
These strikes
bring out the heavyweights.

We talk of escalation,
and at our own meetings
others from the province
bring greetings
and wishes of support – as if we are sick
wrapped up, in hospital,
with a broken leg,
recovering from a fall.

At the back of the hall
someone will cry out
for secret ballot
but there is no time now
for such niceties.
We tolerate
the naysayers and the abstainers
as long as the electric will
runs through us again:
We have the right
to withdraw
our labour.

We have the right...
We have the right...
We have the right.

These words ring in me,
give and take

what I myself might think,
and which later I must find
in the dark before sleep
when the thug of my tongue
is calmed, held down
healed,
lightened.

■ OUR NEGOTIATOR SPEAKS TO THEIRS
DALE ZIEROTH

Let's be clear about this:
this isn't me sitting here
but all of us embodied in me.
I am the tongue for all,
the voice of the group
and I am empowered to say
what they would say,
and what I want, they would want.

I have been chosen
to look you in the eye
and make clear to you at last
that unless you move toward our position
we're not moving toward yours.
Around this table, the water jug,
the styrofoam cups, the loosened ties,
the pads of paper are all
waiting for you.

Yes you're getting paid
and we are not, are in fact
cold and wrestling with sickness
in the dark of the picket line – but let it rain:
the elements will keep us
on track: start with the language
in article 3.04
and then move forward until we stop –
and at that point let us dance
– sometimes you leading, sometimes me,
offering, rejecting,
breaking to rewrite and whisper.

Come now, my colleagues are cold,
and I hear them shuffling and stamping
in the street.

■ CAUGHT IN THE NEWS
DALE ZIEROTH

On the first day of the strike
they drove by honking and giving us
the finger, and we were depressed
until another stranger came by
with doughnuts and coffee and she said
good luck. So we remembered
to be glad that the rain had quit;
yet the cold ran up our legs from the pavement
and bit into us. Our signs flew up in our faces,
the wind rattled at us from the trees,
and we were caught in the news.

After the second day on the line,
we watched ourselves on tv and we heard
Knowlton giving us the finger with his
words and half-words, the way he
smiled and went on to Beirut and
a faraway war. So we read
and by all accounts we were asking for
the overthrow of the government again;
friends called from other provinces:
what did the unions want, and I wanted to say
we were hungry for decency – and no more news.

The third day we were out,
we watched them cross –
and we told ourselves right was still right.
But at night, bringing home anger
to our families, and eating it on the table,
an old indigestible piece of the lamb,
we fall into a sleep and a worry: that the
full new fact-of-the-world is turned loose
on us – and we dream late into the night
for a change in the weather, much less
bitter wind.

Remembrance Day, 1983

■ NOVEMBER
LEONA GOM

*it starts when you do it again after they
said no, it starts when you say We and
know who you mean, and each day you
mean one more.*
■ Marge Piercy

it has always happened somewhere else,
somewhere in history before
they knew better, or somewhere south
where politics means guns
and electrodes on the skull.
if it got closer we just
moved away, there was
always another country, another
province. this time
there is no leaving it
to someone else, someone who is
a better revolutionary.
we have lived here too long
to pretend we are still
tourists taking
notes for a book,
with somewhere safe to go home to.
this time it is ourselves
on the picket lines,
we are cold and frightened and
tired, and changed in a way
we will never forgive.

■ CONTRIBUTORS

ANTLER: b. 1946; "lives in Milwaukee but spends two months alone in the wilderness every year. Factory worker at Harley Davidson and Continental Can. Housepainter. Teacher. Circular deliverer. Assistant to woman with multiple sclerosis. Makes a minimal living now from publication and reading his poems around America trying to live up to Whitman's invocation of the poet as 'itinerant gladness scatterer.'" Books of poems include: *Factory* (City Lights, 1980) and *Last Words* (Ballantine, 1986).

M.R. APPELL: b. 1943; "worked at everything from building houses to mobile homes, from electroplating to engineering." Currently lives in London, Ontario and works at the Weldon Library of the University of Western Ontario. His most recent collection of poems is *Savage Spring* (South Western Ontario Poetry, 1987).

BRAD BARBER: b. 1955; jobs worked include construction, tree planting, newspaper reporting, freelance writing. He has spent more than a year in Central America, and at present is publications co-ordinator for the public information office of Douglas College, New Westminster, BC.

DAVID BEAVER: b. 1951; "quit cab driving in 1975 to go to Mexico." Since then he has taught English as a second language at the University of BC and "currently owns a used bookstore in downtown Vancouver called Albion Books, which has a reasonably good poetry section." His collection of poems is *No Free Rides* (MacLeod & Stewart, 1980).

MICKEY BICKERSTAFF: b. 1946; spent 18 years in a one-person office as bookkeeper/secretary, before attending Simon Fraser University in Burnaby, BC, where she is currently a student.

SADHU BINNING: b. 1947; lives in Burnaby, BC, where he is a part-time postal employee and part-time language teacher. He has co-authored

301

and produced a number of plays about the Indo-Canadian community, and his writing has appeared in most of the major Punjabi magazines published in India and abroad. He has edited an anthology of Canadian Punjabi poetry and is co-editor of *Watan*, a literary and cultural magazine.

WILLIAM BORDEN: b. 1938; teaches writing at the University of North Dakota. "His poems and short stories have appeared in many literary magazines, and his novel, *Superstoe*, was published by Harper & Row in the US and Victor Gollacz in England." He is also a prizewinning playwright.

CAROLYN BORSMAN: b. 1946; her work experiences include "typist, welfare aide, student, cocktail waitress, deckhand, master of arts, food waitress, social service worker, master of science, director of public relations, health facilities planner." She is now a health systems consultant, and lives "on a hobby farm" in Surrey, BC.

KATE BRAID: b. 1947; "after years of unhappy labour as a clerical and childcare worker, Kate stumbled onto a construction site in 1977 and has been labouring (mostly) happily ever since as a journey carpenter." She lives in Vancouver and also teaches carpentry at the BC Institute of Technology. Her poems can be heard on *Split Shift*, an audio cassette of poems and songs from the workplace produced by the Vancouver Industrial Writers' Union and the Vancouver folksong group Fraser Union in 1989.

ROBERT CARSON: b. 1945; has worked 27 years on the San Francisco waterfront. He edited *The Waterfront Writers* (anthology, Harper & Row, 1979), won an Emmy for lyrics (1980) for an ABC documentary, and wrote the musical *'34*, about events leading to the 1934 San Francisco General Strike.

CRAIG CHALLENDER: b. 1946; work experience includes "farming, phlebotomist" (phlebotomy is bloodletting for medicinal purposes), "writers' series co-ordinator, and for the last 12 years, college teaching." He now lives in Farmville, Virginia, and teaches English at Longwood College. His publications include two poetry chapbooks, *The Family* (Stronghold, 1983) and *Dakota Time and Other Times* (James McLaird, 1983).

LEON E. CHAMBERLAIN: b. 1946; a resident of Sterling Heights, Michigan. For 25 years he has been a pipefitter at the Ford Motor Company (and for five years a Master Hypnotist). "He has penned two novels, contributes regularly to blue-collar publications, and has been called a 'long-haired radical' by the *Detroit News*."

PETER CHRISTENSEN: b. 1951; wilderness guide, raconteur, photographer and writer of poetry, stories, biographies and screenplays. He lives in Radium Hot Springs, BC, and his recent collections of poems include *Stalking Place* (Hawk Press) and *To Die Ascending* (Thistledown, 1988).

DAVID R. CONN: b. 1950; "worked five years as a shipbuilder and steel fabricator in Vancouver. He is now a public librarian and freelance writer. A founding member of the Vancouver Industrial Writers' Union, he presently contributes to a regional marine magazine. The poems published here are mainly from *Ticket Stubs for the Bullgang: Poems from the Vancouver Waterfront* (Caitlin, 1980)."

FRANK A. CROSS, JR.: b. 1945; "has worked at many kinds of farm jobs: cotton chopping, cotton picking, hay hauling, irrigating, tractor driving, cow feeding. He has worked as a tractor mechanic and farm equipment welder." At present he lives near Chowchilla, California, where "he farms 160 acres in cotton, corn and wheat." A collection of his Vietnam War poems is *Reminders* (Seven Buffaloes Press, 1986).

ROBERT CURRIE: b. 1937; "was first a labourer, then a pharmacist, before settling in for the long haul as a teacher of English" at a high school in Moose Jaw, Saskatchewan. His recent books include both fiction – *Night Games* (Coteau, 1983) – and poetry – *Learning on the Job* (Oberon, 1986).

JIM DANIELS: b. 1956; "I have worked as a soda jerk, a liquor store clerk, a stockboy in a department store, a janitor, a bank bookkeeper, a short-order cook, and as an assembly line worker in an auto plant. I am currently working as a teacher." He lives in Pittsburgh and his most recent publications include *Digger's Territory* (Adastra, 1989) and *Punching Out* (Wayne State University Press, 1990).

MARY DI MICHELE: b. 1949; "immigrated to Canada from Italy in 1955, working class family; single parent with one daughter." In winter 1990 she was writer-in-residence at Concordia University in Montreal. Her recent poetry collections include *Immune to Gravity* (1986) and *Luminous Emergencies* (1990), both from McClelland and Stewart.

DOUGLAS DOBYNS: b. 1943; has been a commercial fisherman for 15 years. At present he works as a fisheries biologist for a small Indian tribe in northwestern Washington state.

JIM DODGE: b. 1945; "from 1970–85 he lived on an isolated communal homestead in the Coast Range where for five years he was a member of the Cazadero Forest Workers' Co-operative, working mainly as a tree-planter and on stream-clearance projects." He now lives in Arcata, California. His publications include, besides poetry chapbooks, three books of fiction – most recently *Stone Junction* (Atlantic Monthly Press, 1990).

SUE DORO: b. 1937; she "has been writing poetry for 41 years, parenting for 31 years and machining tractor housings and locomotive axles/wheels for 12½ years." She now lives in Oakland, California, "where she works as an advocate for women in blue collar non-traditional trades. Her current job is as an equal opportunity specialist for the US Department of Labour." Her collections of poems include *Of Birds and Factories* (1983) and *Heart, Home and Hard Hats* (Midwest Villages and Voices, 1986).

GLEN DOWNIE: b. 1953; "is a medical social worker in Vancouver, currently working with cancer patients and their families." His books of poems include *An X-Ray of Longing* (Polestar, 1987) and *Heartland* (Mosaic, 1990).

SUSAN EISENBERG: b. 1950; "is a poet, parent, performer, teacher and union electrician (IBEW) in Boston. Having entered construction in the first year of affirmative action guidelines for US women, 1978, she still finds it the most efficient way to pay the bills. Author of the poetry book, *It's a Good Thing I'm Not Macho* (Whetstone, 1984) and the play, *Mother Country*, she has recently completed a performance video, *Coffee Break Secrets*, scripted from poetry about daily work."

KIRSTEN EMMOTT: b. 1947; "lives in Vancouver and works as a mother and a family doctor." Her chapbook of poems is *Are We There Yet?* (Dollarpoems, Brandon University, 1988).

BRETT ENEMARK: b. 1948; "worked in a clothing store, a sawmill, the bush, a ditch, a truck, railroad and highway construction, a library, some gardens and offices. Survived two megaprojects." Currently an engineering aide for the BC Highways Ministry.

DAVID EVEREST: b. 1945; lives near Balfour, BC. He "has been plucked on a variety of jobs since the summer of '62, usually as some kind of 'fixer'. He is currently winning a battle with workaholism during a transition between working as a self-employed micro-sawmill operator and starting a small bread bakery."

LYN FERLO: "b. (apparently); is an artist...who has also become somewhat proficient as a plasterer, wall paper remover, wall board hanger, carpenter, floor sander, painter, paperhanger, floor tile layer, etc. ad nauseum, who intends, when it is All Over, to do very little more than lie on the couch and eat chocolates! In the meantime, she works as a secretary at a major university, the latest in a lifelong string of 'because I need to eat' jobs." She lives in Pittsburgh; her poems also appear in *Overtime* (Piece of the Hunk/West End Press, 1990), the anthology of Pittsburgh's *Mill Hunk Herald* magazine (1979–89).

JEAN FLANAGAN: b. 1946; has held jobs ranging "from dishwasher to secretary, administrator and personnel officer." At present she lives in Arlington, Massachusetts, and works in communications at MIT's nuclear science lab.

JEFF FRIEDMAN: b. 1953; "in my earlier jobs – and there were dozens, including line packer in a welding rod factory, warehouse jobs, nurse's aide, researcher – I held on to the hope that I would find a better work situation. In recent years, I've moved on to various teaching and office positions, and the possibility of finding a healthy work situation seems remote." He lives in Brooklyn; his collection of poems is *The Record-Breaking Heat Wave* (Bookmark, 1986).

ROBERT GARRISON: b. 1947; after occupational and spiritual journeys "arm-wrestling life," that took him from Colorado to the Yukon to Libya, he now lives in Avondale, Arizona, where he teaches flying to Lufthansa pilots-to-be.

LEONA GOM: b. 1946; has been a secretary, waitress, tombstone cutter and teacher, "the latter at levels from Grade One to College." Her most recent books include *Private Properties* (poems; Sono Nis, 1986) and *Zero Avenue* (novel; Douglas & McIntyre, 1989).

MIRIAM GOODMAN: b. 1938; "works on speech recognition applications for computers" in Boston. She also teaches creative and technical writing, and has been a fellow at the Fine Arts Work Center in Provincetown, Massachusetts. Her book of poems is *Signal::Noise* (Alice James Books, 1982).

CHIP GOODRICH: b. 1951; "has worked for the past 15 years as a gardener, for a convent, an orphanage, for private homes, and currently for Benton County Parks in Corvallis, Oregon; supervised County's correction work crew, 1984–87." Other poetry of his is included in the anthology *Season of Dead Water: a Response in Prose and Poetry to the Oil Spill in Prince William Sound* (Breitenbush, 1990).

EVELYN GRAYSON: b. 1949; has been a teacher of high school English and theatre arts since 1974, most recently in Hamilton, Ontario.

JIM GREEN: b. 1941; "worked at everything from a ranch hand to a white collar office worker in the last 30 years." He is a longtime resident of Fort Smith in the Northwest Territories, where his weekly radio show ("Dog River Tales") has run for more than two years. His books of poems include *Beyond Here* (Thistledown, 1983) and he has released an album of his poems set to music with Pat Buckna, *Flint & Steel*.

AL GRIERSON: b. 1948; has been employed as "a journalist, railroader, professional entertainer, builder's laborer and Buddhist monk" in Canada, the US and the British Isles. He now lives in Ashland, Oregon, "where he works as a maker of tofu and folk music."

RICHARD GROSSMAN: b. 1943; "for many years was Pharaoh for a large corporate slave combine, overseeing administration and ritual slaughter." Now lives in Minneapolis, where he works as a "degenerate poet and novelist, writing devotional hymns and nasty street humour." His books of poems include *Tycoon Boy* (1983) and *The Animals* (1983), both from Zygote Press.

DALE HALL: b. 1958; has been a waitress part-time and full-time for the past 15 years. At present she is the sexual harassment adviser at York University in Toronto, and is an adult basic education instructor at the Metro Toronto Labour Education and Skills Training Centre.

PHIL HALL: b. 1953; "has been, among other things, Cupid, Santa, an orderly, a homecare worker and a legal editor. He lives in Toronto, where currently he is a househusband, teacher and freelancer." He co-edits (with Andrew Vaisius) the labour arts "chap-journal" *Don't Quit Yr Day-Job*. His books of poems include *Old Enemy Juice* (Quarry, 1988) and *Amanuensis* (Brick, 1989).

GWEN HAUSER: b. 1944; employment includes "factory jobs, highway jobs, tenant organizing, political/social research and market research." She "is a Torontonian living in Hamilton, Ontario (viz. Toronto as a state of mind)." Her recent collections include *Poems for the Colour Green* (Goldflower, 1986).

LINDA M. HASSELSTROM: b. 1943; grew up on a ranch in western South Dakota. She received an MA in American Literature from the University of Missouri/Columbia before returning to the ranch. She operated a small press for 14 years, and now conducts writing workshops. Her recent books include *Windbreak: A Woman Rancher on the Northern Plains* (journal; Barn Owl Books, 1987) and *Roadkill* (poetry; Spoon River Poetry Press, 1987).

GERALD HILL: b. 1951; "once cleaned up in a Catholic church, then delivered ice to a summer resort area, then taught adult education, and now studies, writes and parents in Edmonton." His collection of poems is *Heartwood* (Thistledown, 1985).

RICHARD HOLINGER: teaches English at Marmion Academy in Aurora, Illinois. He has published poetry and prose in a number of journals, including *Southern Review*, *Chelsea* and *American Book Review*.

BRUCE HUNTER: b. 1952; a high school dropout, "for ten years he worked at a variety of jobs including construction worker, equipment operator, and gardener for Victoria Lawn Cemetery in St. Catharines, Ontario. He went to university at age 29 and now teaches English at Seneca College in Toronto." Poems here are from his books, published by Thistledown, *Benchmark* (1982) and *The Beekeeper's Daughter* (1986).

TODD JAILER: b. 1956; "worked on poles and wires for an electrical utility in Western Pennsylvania. Currently a member of the South End Press publishing collective in Boston." His essays and poems have appeared many places, including *Intifada: The Palestinian Uprising Against Israeli Occupation* (South End, 1989) and Peter Oresick and Nicholas Coles' *Working Classics: Poems on Industrial Life* (University of Illinois Press, 1990).

JANET KAUFFMAN: b. 1945; raised on a tobacco farm. She has published several collections of fiction and poetry, including *Places in the World a Woman Could Walk* (Knopf, 1984), *Collaborators* (Knopf, 1986) and *Obscene Gestures for Women* (Knopf, 1989).

DYMPHNY KOENIG-CLEMENT: b. 1967 in Holland, immigrated to Canada in 1970: "she quit school at age 14, and has worked all kinds of crazy jobs ever since, usually the near-slavery-minimum-wage kind." She was a writer/researcher for an international accounting firm in Holland in 1987–88, and now lives in Victoria, BC, where she works as a freelance editor and writer.

RONALD KURT: b. 1958; "no longer working in shipping and receiving. Saw the light one day (I think) and quit." He now works part time in an Edmonton bookstore. His collections of poems include the chapbook *Voices Controlling the Beasts* (Dollarpoems, Brandon University, 1988) and *Voices from Earth* (with Mark McCawley; Prairie Journal Press, forthcoming).

ZOË LANDALE: b. 1952; "worked for a number of years as a commercial fisher on the BC coast." She now lives in Delta, BC, where "she is a parent, works in the home and writes poetry and freelance journalism." She edited the Vancouver Industrial Writers' Union anthology *Shop Talk* (Pulp Press, 1985) and is a past-president of the Federation of BC Writers.

DONNA LANGSTON: b. 1953; her employment record includes "clerical, waitressing, oil refinery worker, factories." She now lives in Minnesota, where she teaches in a university women studies department. Her books include the women studies textbook *Changing Our Power* (Kendall-Hunt, 1989).

DAVID LEE: b. 1944; now teaches at Southern Utah State College and "lives quietly with Jan, Jon and Jodee in St. George, Utah." His books of poems include *The Porcine Canticles* (1984) and *Day's Work* (1990), both from Copper Canyon Press.

ALISSA LEVINE: b. 1968; "has worked at various grueling jobs from which she has gained an intricate understanding of the socio-econolinguistic implications of sweat: lawn mower denotes either the machine or the person; a waitress is a lawn mower without the machine." She is now a student in French at the University of Winnipeg.

STEPHEN LEWANDOWSKI: b. 1947; lives in Naples, New York, where he is an educator with the Ontario County Soil and Water Conservation

District. His books of poems include *Inside Out* (Crossing, 1979) and *Honey and Ashes* (Tamarack, 1984).

RHONA MCADAM: b. 1957; "has spent a frightening number of years in government offices of one sort or another, but has only filed a grievance once (she won, too). She left that job to become self-employed (as a freelance writer), doing contract work for the government of Alberta, but she believes that's not the same as working for them." Her collections of poems include *Hour of the Pearl* (1987) and *Creating the Country* (1989), both from Thistledown Press.

MARK MCCAWLEY: b. 1964; past jobs include shipper/receiver, photocopier technician, waiter. Most recently he has been a writing teacher, editor, and househusband in Edmonton. His collections of poems include *Last Minute Instructions* (Unfinished Monument, 1989) and *Voices from Earth* (with Ron Kurt; Prairie Journal Press, forthcoming).

DAVID MCKAIN: b. 1937; "has worked in factories, driven truck, dug ditches, been a roofer, carpenter, farmer." He now teaches at the University of Connecticut. His books include *The Common Life* (poetry; AliceJames Books), *Spellbound: Growing Up in God's Country* (nonfiction; Simon & Schuster, 1990) and *Spirit Bodies* (poetry; Ithaca House, 1990).

JIM MCLEAN: b. 1940; "have been with CP Rail for 34 years. Presently assistant superintendent, CP Rail, Winnipeg, Manitoba." Publications include *The Secret Life of Railroaders* (poetry; Coteau, 1982) and *Wildflowers Across the Prairies* (illustrator; Western Producer Prairie Books, 1984).

ROBERT MACLEAN: b. 1948; spent "seven years planting trees in BC with Brinkman Reforestation, tendonitis in hands caused by holding a shovel all day forced me to switch jobs, now (the last three years) university prof in Kyoto, Japan." His books include *Tree Dream Deep* (Brinkman & Associates, 1990), *among what is lost* (Cowan & Tetley, 1988) and *In a Canvas Tent* (Sono Nis, 1984).

TIM MCNULTY: b. 1949; "has worked in the woods and mountains of the Pacific Northwest since he moved there in the early 1970s." He lives in Quilcene, Washington, and now "divides his time between trail work for Olympic National Park and freelance writing." His publications include *Last Year's Poverty* (poems; Brooding Heron, 1987), *As a Heron Unsettles a Shallow Pool* (poems; Exiled-in-America, 1988) and *Washington's Wild Rivers* (prose; The Mountaineers, 1990).

MARJORIE MARKS: b. 1958; has been a waitress, executive secretary, "PBX operator." She currently teaches middle school language arts and drama in a Detroit suburb.

SID MARTY: b. 1944: after more than a decade as a park warden in Canada's mountain national parks, he is presently a full-time writer of prose and poetry in Calgary and Lundbreck, Alberta. His publications include *Men for the Mountains* (non-fiction, McClelland and Stewart, 1978), *Nobody Danced with Miss Rodeo* (poetry; McClelland & Stewart, 1981) and *A Grand and Fabulous Notion: The First Century of Canada's Parks* (history; NC Press, 1984).

JOSEPH MAVIGLIA: b. 1953; lives in Toronto, where he works in construction. His collection of poems is *Movietown* (Streetcar Editions, 1989).

SUSAN MEURER: b. 1943; "is a printer by trade. Her work led to union involvement in occupational health and safety. More recently, she has worked as a freelance writer and researcher." She lives in Toronto, where her experience with workers displaced by plant closures was the basis for a musical, *Shadowboxers*, also broadcast on CBC radio.

SUZAN MILBURN: b. 1954; jobs include "swimming instructor, group leader, baker and deli person. She presently works at a French pre-school in Vernon, BC, and teaches creative writing at night."

RON MILES: b. 1944; now Dean of Arts and Education, Cariboo College, Kamloops, BC. Earlier, he taught for 15 years at Cariboo and at the University of Alberta. His collection of poems is *These People* (Harbour, 1984).

JONI MILLER: b. 1955; her various jobs include factory work, secretary, and rape crisis counselor. "These days she works at graphic arts and teaches karate" in Vancouver. Her collection of poems is *These Are the Women* (MacLeod Books, 1981).

JOHN MORTON: formerly worked at the lead-zinc smelter in Trail, BC. He was last reported living in Berkeley, California; the editor and publisher would be very grateful for any information as to his current whereabouts.

ERIN MOURÉ: b. 1955; has been for many years an employee of VIA Rail, including waitress and service manager. She has lived and worked in Montreal since 1985. Her books include *Wanted Alive* (1983), *Domestic Fuel* (1985), and *Furious* (1988, winner of the Governor General's Award), all from Anansi. Most recently she published *WSW (West South West)* with Véhicule, 1989.

NICK MUSKA: b. 1942; lives in Toledo, Ohio, where after his stint in warehousing he now teaches writing at the county jail and a prison farm. His collections of poems are *ELM: Warehouse Poems* (1979) and *Living My Nightlife Out Under the Sun* (1987), both from Toledo Poets Center Press.

LESLÉA NEWMAN: b. 1955; worked as a secretary at various offices for many years. Currently she lives in Northhampton, Massachusetts, and runs "Write from the Heart: Writing Workshops for Women." She has written fiction and poetry, and edited the anthology *Bubbe Meisehs by Shayneh Maidelehs: An Anthology of Poetry by Jewish Granddaughters About Our Grandmothers*.

MIKE O'CONNOR: b. 1944; for 10 years farmed on the Olympic Peninsula, while also working "as a treeplanter, hand/horse logger, woodcutter, and forester." For the past nine years he has written and edited for the China Economic News Service in Taipei, Taiwan. His most recent book of poems is *The Basin: Life in a Chinese Province* (Empty Bowl, 1988).

JAMIE PEARSON: b. 1959; "I attended the University of Windsor after travelling around doing blue-collar jobs. I left university before finishing anything because I had to work. I have been unemployed most of my adult life." Currently lives in Vancouver. "When I can dig up the spare change, I still buy the odd lottery ticket."

PENNY PIXLER: b. 1947; "after I got out of electronics school, in order to get my female foot into the industry, I worked odd shifts in airplane-hangar-like factories." She lives and works in Chicago, debugging circuit boards and "still trying to write SciFi."

JEFF PONIEWAZ: b. 1946; a Milwaukee eco-activist, whose "collected ecological poems and meditations" is *Dolphin Leaping in the Milky Way* (Inland Ocean Books, 1986). He teaches an off-campus course on ecological visionary literature for the University of Wisconsin, but "nowadays his most frequent foreman is the Muse."

BRIAN PRATT: b. 1956; has spent "almost ten years fussing and a-fuming" as a bus driver in Vancouver for BC Transit. Previous work experience includes being a security "Nazi" (Pinkerton's), "turkey catcher" (Panco Poultry), "getting behind on MacDonald Cedar's green chain" (sawmill) and a wonderful year "working for the government" (unemployment).

ALICIA PRIEST: b. 1953; for many years worked as a Registered Nurse in hospitals throughout BC. After making the switch from nursing to newspaper journalism, she is at present the *Vancouver Sun*'s medical reporter.

KEN RIVARD: b. 1947; "has worked at various jobs including moving company helper, office boy, messenger, university teaching and CPR policeman." He currently works as a special education teacher in a Calgary elementary school. His most recent books include *Frankie's Desires* (poems; Quarry, 1987) and *Working Stiffs* (short fiction; Greensleeves Publishing, 1990).

TIMOTHY RUSSELL: b. 1951; is an apprentice millwright in the boiler repair department of the steel mill in which he has worked since 1973. His home is in Toronto, Ohio, and he has two poetry chapbooks: *The Possibility of Turning to Salt* and *In Dubio* (State Street Press, 1988).

PAT ERWIN SALYER: b. 1945; grew up on Muddy Creek in East Tennessee. She has worked for a book manufacturer, as a Baptist church secretary and as a telephone operator. Currently she lives in Kingsport, Tennessee, and is employed by a market research firm.

ROBERT W. SANDFORD: b. 1949; "is a naturalist, corporate communications consultant and writer who works out of Canmore, Alberta. He has published two books on natural history."

BRUCE SEVERY: b. 1947; currently edits interactive instructional software in Santa Monica, California.

CATHERINE SHAW: b. 1950; "started working in secretarial jobs in 1968. In 1979 she finally rose through the ranks and became a book editor. Now, furiously backpedaling, she works as an executive secretary for a major financial institution. She was born, and continues to live and work, in New York City."

SANDY SHREVE: b. 1950; worked in public libraries in the 1970s. For the past 10 years she has been employed by Simon Fraser University in Burnaby, BC, where she is currently program assistant for Women's Studies. She edited *Working for a Living* (1988), a special issue of the magazine *Room of One's Own*. Her collection of poems is *The Speed of the Wheel is Up to the Potter* (Quarry, 1990).

SUE SILVERMARIE: b. 1947; "has worked for the Postal Service as a night shift machine clerk sorting 60 letters/minute in a factory environment, as a window clerk in a rural Appalachian post office gossip center, and as city carrier." Now she lives in Milwaukee, where she is a social worker in a nursing home, and has a private practice in poetry therapy with the elderly. She recently was the subject of a poetry video, *Look Mama the Mailman is a Girl*.

GLEN SORESTAD: b. 1937; taught elementary and high school for more than 20 years, including 12 years as an English teacher at a Saskatoon, Saskatchewan collegiate. He is presently a full-time writer and publisher. His nine books of poems include *Hold the Rain in Your Hands* (Coteau, 1985) and a collection of his short stories, *The Windsor Hotel*, is forthcoming.

RICHARD STANSBERGER: b. 1950; "is a third-generation steel worker." After working at various other jobs, he currently teaches English in a Cincinnati high school. His most recent collection of poems is *In the White of the Last Thought* (Heartsblood, 1986).

CLEMENS STARCK: b. 1937; "probably one of the few Princeton alumni to have made a career of manual labour." A long-time union carpenter, his poems have appeared in numerous magazines and he has given readings throughout the Northwest. He presently works as a carpenter for Oregon State University and "lives in the foothills of the Coast Range, south of Dallas, Oregon."

JEFF TAGAMI: b. 1954; "worked in the fields, orchards, packing sheds and lumber mills of the Pajaro Valley in Watsonville, California." At present he lives in San Francisco and works in the administrative services department of a leasing company. Book of poems: *October Light* (Kearney Street Workshop Press, 1987).

ROGER TAUS: b. 1941; jobs include short-order cook, dishwasher, telephone company frameman, metal cutter in a scrapyard, freeze dryer operator in a plasma fractionation factory, lotion compounder in a cosmetics factory, editor and technical writer. Currently he lives in Los Angeles, where he is a proofreader for a daily newspaper. His collections of poems are *Trophies of the Sun* (El Corno Emplumado, 1964) and *Poems from the Combat Zone* (Tao Anarchy Books, 1984).

PAM TRANFIELD: b. 1960; "bounced between government-funded jobs and unemployment insurance claims until she was put on the federal payroll as a clerk. She endured two years in the commission, and has since found peace as a member-worker in a Vancouver natural foods wholesale co-operative." She is a member of the Vancouver Industrial Writers' Union.

PETER TROWER: b. 1930; was a logger on BC's coast for 22 years. Also worked as a shakecutter, smelter hand, surveyor, janitor, laundryman and pulp mill labourer. Became a professional writer in 1972. His books of poetry include *The Slidingback Hills* (Oberon, 1986) and *Unmarked Doorways* (Harbour, 1989).

MICHAEL B. TURNER: b. 1962; "grew up in the west coast fishing industry, where I worked as a butcher-grader and a tallyman. Currently I am playing in the Hard Rock Miners, a Vancouver-based 'citybilly' band."

ANDREW VAISIUS: b. 1950; jobs include laboratory analyst in the pharmaceutical industry. He now directs an inner city day care centre in Winnipeg.

M.C. WARRIOR: b. 1952; has been both a BC coast logger and fisherman, and has been an organizer with the United Fishermen and Allied Workers Union. Currently he is working on labour history projects. His collection of poems is *Quitting Time* (MacLeod Books, 1978).

TOM WAYMAN: b. 1945; work experience includes various blue- and white-collar jobs in Canada and the US, including motor truck assembly and (for the past 14 years) college teaching. His books include *Going for Coffee* (work poems anthology, 1981), *Inside Job: Essays on the New Work Writing* (1983) and *In a Small House on the Outskirts of Heaven* (poems, 1989), all from Harbour.

CALVIN WHARTON: b. 1952; has been employed at a range of jobs, "some more satisfying than others, and few he would categorize as *fun*." Now living in Nelson, BC, he "is enjoying teaching writing and editing at Selkirk College." His most recent publication is *East of Main: An Anthology of Poems from East Vancouver* (co-edited with Tom Wayman; Pulp Press, 1989) and his chapbook of poems is *Visualized Chemistry* (Tsunami, 1987).

HOWARD WHITE: b. 1945; worked construction around BC from 1965 on, mostly as a cat operator. He currently runs Harbour Publishing, edits the journal *Raincoast Chronicles*, and is a best-selling oral historian. Books include *Spilsbury's Coast* and *The Accidental Airline* (oral history; Harbour), his collection of poems, *The Men There Were Then* (Pulp Press, 1982), *A Hard Man to Beat* (oral history, Pulp Press) and most recently *Writing in the Rain* (prose and poetry, Harbour, 1990).

FINN WILCOX: "lives with his family on the Olympic Peninsula in Washington state, where he has been a tree planter since 1975. He, along with his wife and several others, run Empty Bowl press in Port Townsend." His publications include *Working the Woods, Working the Sea: An Anthology of Northwest Writers* (co-edited with Jeremiah Gorsline; Empty Bowl, 1986).

ANDREW WREGGITT: b. 1955; raised in a small mining town in northern BC. "Worked in the mine several times and at many other assorted jobs. Has spent the last six years as a full-time writer, mostly in film and television." His most recent collection of poems is *Making Movies* (Thistledown, 1989).

DALE ZIEROTH: b. 1946; teaches at Douglas College in New Westminster, BC, where he edits the literary journal, *Event*. He lives in North Vancouver, BC, with his wife and two daughters. His most recent book of poems is *When the Stones Fly Up* (Anansi, 1985).